'A VOICE IN THE WILDERNESS'

'A VOICE IN THE WILDERNESS'

Further teachings from Silver Birch

Edited by

TONY ORTZEN

The Spiritual Truth Press

First published in 1986
Reprinted 2000

Spiritual Truth Press
15 Broom Hall, Oxshott
Surrey KT22 0JZ

ISBN 0 85384 109 8

Printed in Great Britain by Booksprint

FOREWORD

There are a number of possible reasons why you are reading this book. The first and most likely is that you are already a 'follower' of Silver Birch and have found his great wisdom and spiritual insights of benefit in your life. In this case you will welcome this reprint of one of the classic books of his teachings. Maybe you have been given this book by a friend who believes its message of love, in this world and the next, will inspire or comfort you. If so, you will not be dissappointed.

Perhaps you chanced upon it on a bookshelf or saw it advertised, then curiosity got the better of you. Well, after reading its pages you may also decide that 'chance' played no part in the decision and that some form of spiritual guidance has brought you and this book together.

Whatever the reason, the chances are that Silver Birch's wisdom will remain with you forever. Long after you have forgotten his precise words, his guidance will still be a very real influence whenever you need it. And if you need to jog your memory - just reach for this book and read it again. Silver Birch's words are so accessible and meaningful that you will never tire of reading them. But who is Siver Birch, the spirit guide whose words are faithfully recorded here? And who was Maurice Barbanell, the London medium who channelled that wisdom? Without an answer to these qestions, many new readers - however impressed with these teachings - will be puzzled about their source.

Barbanell was the founder and editor of a weekly Spiritualist newspaper, *Psychic News*, and for half a century devoted his life to spreading spiritual knowledge through its columns and those of other publications with which he was associated. In his own obituary, which he wrote before his passing at the age of 79 on July 17th

1981, he revealed that he was told by Estelle Roberts' Red Cloud - a spirit guide for whom he had the greatest admiration - that in a previous incarnation he had made a promise to reincarnate and devote his life to spreading Spiritualism. Though he had no knowledge of that life or promise, events certainly conspired to make it possible.

He was born to Jewish parents in a poor area of London's East End. His mother was devoutly religious but his father, a barber, was an atheist so Barbanell heard many arguments about religion during his early years. His father always won, and his son adopted the same outlook but later changed to agnosticism. Yet after hearing about Spiritualism from a speaker at a social and literary club of which he was secretary, Barbanell refused to start the debate by putting an opposing view - one of his duties - because, he explained, he had made no personal investigation and therefor his opinions were valueless. This impressed the speaker who invited Barbanell to attend a sceance in which a medium, Mrs Blaustein, was entranced by various spirits of different nationalities. He was not impressed, and on a second visit fell asleep. Barbanell apologised, believing that either boredom or tiredness had been responsible, but the other circle members informed him that he had not been asleep but had been in trance and a Red Indian had spoken through him.

With the enccouragement of famous Fleet Street journalist Hannen Swaffer, Barbanell founded *Psychic News* partly as a vehicle for the guide's teachings. But, because he knew he would be criticised for publishing his own mediumship in his own newspaper, Barbanell did not reveal to his readers for many years who was channelling the wisdom, by which time the guide had a huge following on his own merits.

Silver Birch spoke regularly at Barbanell's home circle and the proceedings were always recorded in shorthand. There were a number of diffferences in style and procedure between Barbanell's own journalistic efforts and the way in which Silver Birch communicated, as Barbanell himself observed: "In my working life I use words every day. I have never yet written or dictated an article with which I was satisfied when I read it. Inevitably I find, when looking at the typed material, that I can improve it by altering words, phrases and sentences. No such problem arises with the guide'steachings. These flow perfectly, requiring usually only punctuation. Another interesting aspect is the occasional use of words that I regard as archaic and do not form part of my normal vocabulary."

But who was Silver Birch? A psychic artist depicts him as a serious-looking native American Indian with a single feather and compassionate eyes. There is evidence to suggest that this was simply a convenient *persona* behind which a far more spiritually-evolved soul hid in order that those who read his words would judge them not by the name attached to them but by the wisdom that pervades every sentence.

Those of us who knew both were well aware of the differences in the way they spoke and the words they used. They both had spiritual missions and they fulfilled them admirably, particularly when working together in their unique two-world partnership. This, as you are about to discover, has provided us with simple, uplifting, comforting and inspirational answers to the questions we all ask, from time to time, about life and its purpose. They are needed now more than ever before as we prepare for the challenges that will confront us in the 21st century.

Roy Stemman
Chairman
Spiritual Truth Foundation

CONTENTS

INTRODUCTION

IS it wrong to kill animals for food and clothes? Should mediums be vegetarians? What is the most urgent reform necessary for the world? Are new souls constantly being born? Does a germ have consciousness? Are guides specifically appointed to their earthly charges?

Questions, questions, questions! And how Silver Birch, the guide of Hannen Swaffer's home circle, loved and thrived upon them.

For decades visitors from throughout the world went to Maurice Barbanell's flat to hear the guide speak through his superb trance mediumship. Some were famous in their chosen paths or vocations. But the majority were ordinary folk, fellow travellers along a spiritual pilgrimage, all searching for the truth.

Silver Birch never once showed impatience, intolerance, annoyance or anger. Neither did he judge those who gathered weekly—and later monthly—to hear his words of wisdom, eloquently expressed words which have brought him respect and admiration the world over.

Much of the material in this book has been unavailable for decades. Some, however, originally appeared in two of A. W. Austen's books, "Home Circle," published in 1940, and "Spirit Guidance," which appeared one year later.

Most, I should explain, has been carefully selected from the archives of "Psychic News" in which the guide's words frequently appeared in the early days of his circle.

Truly has it been a labour of love and loyalty to read, digest and marry together in a cohesive form the guide's superb teachings. How wonderful it is to breathe new life into yellowing, long forgotten cuttings, sure in the knowledge that Silver Birch's philosophy cannot age or tarnish or his language lose its lustre.

Most of the home circle members have now passed beyond earthly gaze or are in the autumn of their lives. This book is therefore dedicated to that noble band of men and women who sat patiently and willingly for years, forging a vital bridge between the Seen and Unseen, the living and the so-called dead.

"Cast away all the old fables," said Silver Birch. "Discard foolish superstition; free yourselves from prejudice. All those things obscure your vision and cramp your mind. Be tolerant, humble, ready to receive revelations from the divine fountain of wisdom. To all who read these words, 'Go thou and do likewise'."

His message is as relevant now as ever it was. And so it will remain until long after we, too, have ended life's journey and entered the glorious spiritual realms whence he came . . .

Tony Ortzen

Chapter One

'TO DIE IS NOT TRAGIC'

AT some time in life all must face death, whether it be the passing of a loved one, a friend, neighbour, colleague or acquaintance. For a sad few it is a shattering experience, from which it may take months—or years—to recover. How blessed are Spiritualists who have a faith and inner conviction which can be backed up by demonstrable evidence that all survive so-called death.

"To die is not tragic," said Silver Birch. "To live in your world is tragic. To see the garden of the Great Spirit choked with the weeds of selfishness and greed and avarice, that is tragedy.

"To 'die' is to enjoy freedom of the spirit, which has been imprisoned behind the bars of the material body. Is it tragic to be released from suffering, for the soul to come into its own? Is it tragic to see wonders of colour, to hear music that does not belong to material expression?

"Is it tragic for repressed genius to find the means of expressing its latent gifts? Is it tragic to live in a world where there is no selfishness, no greed, where there is no money to hinder the growth of the soul? Do you call that tragic?

"Do you call it tragic to express yourself in a body that has no pain, to be able to roam all over the world of matter in a flash and to taste the beauties of the spirit life too?"

Once Silver Birch explained to those present that those on earth frequently visited the spirit world in the sleep state "otherwise it would be such a shock when you came here to start your real life in earnest."

"When we pass on, shall we remember our visits during sleep?" asked a sitter.

"Yes, of course," said the guide, "because you will then be freed from the limitation of the body and you will be able to express in the full all the consciousness which has been released during your sleep. In its new expression, it will bring to you all the memories that you have, the memories of all the experiences that you have enjoyed."

Silver Birch was asked about the position of those who, after passing, went to the lower planes of spirit life. Would they remember their sleep visits—presumably to the lower planes—and would that memory help them to adjust their position?

"Those who would gravitate to the lower planes go to those planes during sleep," he replied, "but the memory of that would not help them to realise their position after 'death' because the planes on which they found themselves would still resemble the material world.

"The lower in the world of spirit, the more earthly it is in appearance because the vibrations are more gross; the higher in the realm of spirit, the finer the vibrations."

"Do we sometimes remember our sleep adventures in this life?" asked a sitter, recalling that sometimes he had a vague memory of an experience.

"When your spirit is released from its body, you are freed from your brain, which is your limitation in the world of matter," said Silver Birch. "The consciousness now has experiences on our vibrations, according to your grade of evolution, and it is conscious of its experiences while it has them.

"But, when you go back to your body of matter and try to capture the experiences of the spirit, you cannot do so because one is greater than the other. The smaller cannot hold the greater and you get distortion.

"It is as if you had a little bag and you tried to get lots of things into it. You could only get some of the things into the bag, and the more you pushed the more out of shape they would become.

"That is what happens to you when you return to your bodies. But, if your soul is already evolved and you have reached an advanced stage of consciousness, then you are aware of the spirit realms. Then you can quite easily train the brain to remember.

"I talk with all of you and I often say, 'Remember this when you go back to your world,' but you do not. I have been with each one of you and taken you to many places. But, though you do not remember it now, none of it is ever wasted."

"Do you mean that the memory of these experiences will help us when we pass on?" he was asked.

"Yes," was the reply. "Nothing is wasted. The law is perfect. Those of us who have lived for many years marvel at the perfection of the law, and when we hear the puny minds of your world criticise the Great Spirit—how little they know! The less they know, the more they express themselves."

Silver Birch was asked whether many people were engaged in working during their sleep state or if the visits were used solely for preparation for the larger life.

"Some of you do work," he replied, "because there are many that you can help in your sleep state. But, usually, it is a preparation. You are taken to those places which will help you to be ready for your work when you leave the world of matter. If that were not done, the shock of coming from one sphere of expression to another would be so great that it would take you a long time to recover.

"That is why it is easier for those who have knowledge when they come to our world. Others have to sleep and rest for a long time, until they can adjust themselves. If you have knowledge, then you pass from one state to another and you are aware of the new life. After all, it is just like opening a door and coming into the sunshine. You must get accustomed to the light.

"Those without knowledge would have to have a long period of rest to recover from the period of transition. It is the same as a baby in your world. It has to feel its way. They would still remember their experiences, but more as you remember dreams.

"Nothing is ever lost, in your world or in mine. Always remember that. Every thought, every action, every desire to serve that is thrown out of your hearts, it helps someone somewhere. Always, when the desire is there, you attract those who can help you . . .

"The world is full of darkness. There hang over it the mists of superstition, error and ignorance. The spirit of God has few instruments through which it can be expressed.

"The voice of the prophet is not heard in the land. The open vision has been banished, the sacred instruments driven out. Priestcraft and vested interests have supplanted the inspiration of the living God.

"Materialism has raised its proud head in a denial of all spiritual truths; its gospel has been triumphant, but its results were a world catastrophe accompanied by needless bloodshed, misery, heart-burnings, weariness, sickness of mind, despair, desolation, chaos and confusion.

"The Great Spirit cannot be made silent, and His truths are being proclaimed once again, their object being to restore sanity to a mad world."

Then, in these words Silver Birch explained the purpose of spirit return:

"We seek to drive out misery, fear and desperation. We seek to bring the light of simple truth and reason, the voice of inspiration, of revelation, the wisdom of the spirit that has been crushed, stifled and repressed for too long.

"We seek to bring the spirit back into its proper perspective, so that spiritual powers shall be made manifest and all the faults of a crude materialism be exposed so that for ever they may be discarded.

"We seek to oppose all those vested interests of state, church, nation, class and sect. We seek to bring freedom to all, freedom in its fullest, highest, deepest and purest meaning.

"We seek to abolish the fear and the terror of death, so that all may realise that it has its place in the eternal scheme of life.

"We seek to abolish all the obstacles that stand between the two states of existence, that man may find his soul and in finding his soul find himself. We seek to quicken all the powers of the divine within, so that the Great Spirit shall be expressed through all His children."

Then came these words, obviously addressed to Spiritualists the world over who are fighting for the recognition of spiritual truths:

"You are all the heralds of the new age. You will pay the price of being pioneers, but you will leave behind you a priceless heritage.

"Serve, serve, serve wherever you can. Forget self. Seek to rise above the limitations of puny, materialistic self-interest. Seek to express to the fullest those gifts with which you have been endowed, using them in the fullest service that you all can render.

"We will bring you evidence of our purpose, our mission. We will demonstrate to you that the ones you love most dearly, your own beloved dead, are ranged by our side, so that you shall know that they co-operate with us in the desire to spread truth.

"Behind them we stand, and behind us stand all the lovers of freedom, who belong to all races and all nationalities, who desire to aid you and to serve you.

"And behind us all stands the greatest power in the

universe, the Oversoul of all life, the Divine Architect, the King of all kings, the Great Spirit Whom you call God."

Silver Birch spoke of his visit to the inner spheres of the spirit world at Easter, when a conference of guides was held —as always happened at Easter and Christmas.

"There is no turning back from the tasks in which we are engaged," he said.

"In all our counsels, in all our discussions, in all our efforts to prevent your frenzied, mad world from destroying itself, we seek to point to those paths of truth and freedom and simplicity and wisdom which will enable you to find yourselves and to solve for yourselves all the problems which you have created, and so earn that peace on earth which can still, and will, be obtained by the combination of people of good will labouring together for a common purpose.

"We do not falter in hours of difficulty. We stress the note of optimism and say we are on the side of the Great Spirit. Our aim is to serve. We cannot fail because the Great Spirit cannot fail.

"For millions of years, long before even man trod on your planet, the Law of the Great Spirit was made manifest. His purpose was set in motion and there were brought into your world creatures endowed with His divinity, to play their part in shaping His creation.

"They were given free will, so that as they progressed spiritually and mentally they would learn to use their free will in that mighty purpose.

"The perfect Intelligence, which set the whole universe in motion and endowed inanimate matter with life-giving force and gave consciousness to man, cannot fail, even though the creatures He has created try to thwart His purpose.

"Man cannot see into the mind of the Great Spirit, but the Great Spirit can see into the minds of all men. He is not deceived. All the innermost secrets of every heart are laid

naked and bare before His gaze. Those who cheat themselves
do not cheat the Great Spirit, for His laws cannot be mocked
or set on one side.

"Men may delay His purpose and for a time act as
impediments, but they cannot stay the Divine Plan.

"And so, like many others, I return to you with the
determination to increase our efforts to reinforce with new
hope and zeal and enthusiasm all those who labour for
humanity.

"Many of them have grown grey in this service; their backs
are bending under the load that they have carried. Sometimes
they fear they have accomplished so little, but they are not the
judges of the work that they do. There is only one Judge, Who
judges all things with impartial scales.

"We return because we love you, because we desire to serve
you. There is no other reason. Many of the joys and beauties
to which we are accustomed are not lightly surrendered, but
we relinquish them because there is a greater task for each one
of us."

Accepting that the "dead" can and do return, a young Fleet
Street journalist asked Silver Birch why spirit communicators
had "to manifest in what seem to be such strange and curious
ways." He was referring to sitting in the dark and seance
trumpets. These megaphone-like devices were used to amplify
spirit voices.

"Why is the darkness curious?" asked Silver Birch. "God
made the night and the day. Why should it be more curious to
sit in the dark than in the light? The darkness belongs to the
Great Spirit as does the light, and is not the darkness merely
an absence of light?"

"Yes, but sitting in the dark deprives us of the use of one of
our physical senses," said the visitor.

"It does," admitted the guide, "but it stimulates your
spiritual senses, which unfortunately are seldom exercised in

your world. Must all that is spiritual be reduced to material terms? Must always the heights of inspiration, spiritual truth and wisdom be made physical before you, who are both physical and spiritual, can appreciate their beauties?

"Is it our fault that you cannot respond to the highest and purest vibrations of spirit? Is it our fault that we have to use trumpets to make replicas of earthly voices because you cannot hear the voice of the spirit? Is that a criticism of us or is it a criticism of your world?

"Here we are, real beings, and here are you, spiritual beings with as much spiritual essence as we possess, yet you cannot see, you cannot hear unless we make ourselves semi-visible.

"And then, when we do it to attract your attention, we are told, Why must you do it? Only because your world is so engrossed in matter that it cannot raise itself above material things. If it could, then all the beauty of the world of spirit would be at your command.

"It is not our fault. We would strive to respond to the highest that is within you, but how seldom it is that the highest in you is called into being. How often is the Great Spirit within His children expressed? How often are those finer spiritual qualities brought into manifestation in your world?

"How often does the spirit of altruism and idealism find expression? Is it not too true that more often selfishness rules and materialism is at the helm? These are criticisms of your world, not ours, and we strive to help you to find the eternal realities buried beneath material coverings.

"We would rather do it in a spiritual manner, by inspiration, by touching your souls. We tried. There were so few that could be reached! But if we bang a table, if we make a rap, if a trumpet moves, then your world says, 'How wonderful'—and we say, 'How foolish.' Is it considered more important to make a rap than to stir a soul?"

Then the visitor put his problem to the guide. "Sometimes I get very impatient with the world and its inequalities," he said. "I want to go out and fight—and somehow I never seem able to. What can I do?"

"Let me answer you in my way," said Silver Birch. "To all who live in your world, rich or poor, high or low, irrespective of rank, title, degree, profession or calling, to all there come opportunities for service. It may be a little wrong that has to be redressed, a little inequality that has to be levelled out, a little darkness where you could take the light.

"Do not imagine that the big fights, the ones that receive the glamour of publicity, are the only fights that matter. We see your lives in terms of service, and each can render service. Wherever you may be, your opportunities for service are boundless.

"Strive to give service. Fill your mind, your heart, your soul with that desire, and then automatically you will call to your aid those in my world who are seeking for instruments like you, and you will succeed in being the means whereby the power of the spirit will be expressed through you. And you will then have more to do than you can manage! But it is not a bed of roses you are asking for."

"I do not expect it to be," said the journalist.

"I know," said the guide. "But you will get the satisfaction that springs from within the soul, that sees through the façade of glittering nothings. You see the wasted power, the frittered opportunities, and you know what could be accomplished.

"This seance seems strange to you because it is new to you, but I am obeying a natural law of the universe. Your scientists have not discovered all the laws of the Great Spirit. Their knowledge is infinitesimal. There is a realm of law and knowledge waiting for them when they can aspire to reach it.

"Not all of it will be discovered in laboratories, by scalpels or by instruments of measurement. Some if it can only be truly appreciated by souls that are evolved, minds that are spiritually ready for higher wisdom.

"Knowledge is not arrogant, but humble, for it knows there is greater knowledge to be achieved. Only ignorance is arrogant, for it does not know. The greatest philosophers were always full of humility, for the more they knew the more they realised there was to be known.

"Those who point the finger of scorn and contempt at us are empty-headed and ignorance fills their beings. But the simple souls who desire to know, whose minds are ready for new truths, the power of the spirit can touch, for they are prepared. They are the ones who are of the greatest use to us who are the messengers of the Great Spirit, striving to reveal His knowledge and His wisdom, His power and His will.

"We seek nothing for ourselves. We only desire that you should realise the infinite bounty that you could have, not only in the world of matter, in material things, but in the realm of the mind and the soul, the priceless truths that are waiting for you.

"Selfishness, ignorance and vested interests—these are the forces that stand in the way, and to those we are opposed. We desire to smash them, so that all over your world, wherever there are hungry souls and hungry bodies and hungry minds, there shall be food for them.

"We desire to uplift the weak and the fallen, give strength to the helpless. We desire to rid your world of starvation, illness and sickness. We desire to abolish all foul slums and evil habitations that are a pestilence and a blot on your world.

"We desire to bring light to those who are in darkness, knowledge to those who are ignorant. We desire to lift mankind up, to free him from slavery of mind, body and soul. We desire to fight all selfishness, the poison that saps at your civilisation and brings in its train chaos, bankruptcy, war and destruction.

"We desire to revive the power of the spirit in your midst, that all may seek to live for one another, to co-operate for each other's well-being, to destroy all boundaries founded on hate, greed, avarice and self-interest, so that peace and plenty may be yours as they were intended to be.

"That is our mission, and we are succeeding. If it is to be accomplished by voices speaking in the darkness, so let it be. But the messengers do not matter, the means of communication are unimportant. It is the message that is vital, because it is of God and it will endure.

"Worldly things will disappear, the temporal is but temporal after all. But the realities of the spirit are eternal. Those who pin their faith to the shadowy, intangible material world and its possessions are clutching at shadows. Those who seek the reality of spiritual truths in all their fullness are the ones who are receiving out of life that which is theirs if they would but grasp it. Go forward. Seek knowledge—that precious jewel of the Great Spirit.

"Do not think of me as a voice in the darkness. Think of me as the symbol of eternal spiritual reality. I am nothing; for myself I ask nothing; it is the message I strive to bring. That message is very important; it is the most important thing in your world today.

"All else has failed. Churches, statesmen, scientists, philosophers—none has saved your world. Many in their blindness have brought it nearer and nearer its collapse and almost its destruction. Spiritual truth and spiritual reality can save you, by showing you how to save yourselves.

"Life is not to be found in the world of matter. Its reality is spiritual. Those who deny spiritual truths are denying the life force and if they refuse to make themselves accessible to the power which makes them live they are the sufferers, for they are cutting off the channel."

'Thou art the Great Spirit of all'

"Oh, Great White Spirit, from time immemorial Thy children have sought to understand Thee and Thy purpose. They have tried to trace Thee in the storm, in the thunder, in the lightning.

"They have depicted Thee as a jealous and angry God, full of vindictiveness, desiring the shedding of blood. They have revealed Thee as a partisan Spirit Who seeks to give strength to one and weakness to another, victory to one and defeat to another.

"They have shown Thee as a God of their own religion, and they have attempted to confine Thee within the narrow bounds of their own limitations.

"But we who return in Thy name today seek to reveal Thee as the infinite Spirit of all life, Who art universal Law in all its operations and in all its manifestations. We seek to reveal Thee as the Great Spirit that is in all and through all and without Whose power naught exists.

"We seek to reveal Thee in every phase of life, whether it be those phases known in the world of matter or those higher manifestations of life that are to be found in the realms of spirit.

"We seek to show that Thou art the Great Spirit of all, that in Thy domain there is no boundary between matter and spirit, and Thou reignest over all, seeking to make Thy children realise their kinship with Thee and the power of Thy spirit which is latent within themselves, so that in recognising their divinity they may learn to express the Great Spirit in their lives and rise to the heights of which they are capable, and so become instruments in Thy service.

"To this end we pray and we labour. This is the prayer of Thy Indian servant, who seeks to serve."

Chapter Two

'LIKE THE MIGHTY RAGING WIND'

A MEMBER of Parliament, who lost his wife a few years previously and was seeking evidence of her survival, attended one sitting and had a long and helpful talk with Silver Birch. The MP performed much work in connection with preventing suffering to animals. He went away with a sense of upliftment after being urged to continue his services for reform.

"In your world of matter there is little desire for an understanding of spiritual truths, except among the few of discernment, until sorrow comes," Silver Birch told him.

"But how can I have that discernment?" asked the guest.

"It is not easy," confessed the guide. "You must satisfy yourself, as you have striven to do, that we who speak to you by this and other means are what we claim to be. We can only prove it by conforming to the standard of evidence that your world of matter demands. You must seek that evidence, as you have been seeking it, and judge and weigh with honest criticism what it is that is given to you. If you allow the door to be kept open and yourself provide no *unreasoning* scepticism, you make the channel easy."

"What I simply crave for," the MP said, "is definite knowledge that those who have left this sphere are still living and are in touch with one and are endeavouring to influence one. What must I do to acquire that knowledge?"

"You must use a medium who is better than mine at receiving all those vibrations which will bring you the wholehearted evidence that you require. It is not your soul that demands the knowledge. It is your mind which is agitating in uncertainty."

"Then is there any means whereby I can place my mind more in conscious touch with my soul?"

"That is a question of unfoldment. That is a question of learning how to tune in to the realm of spirit, so that those finer vibrations can become clearer to you."

"How does one tune in?" the visitor wanted to know.

"The activity of your world is often the silence of ours, but the silence of your world is the activity of ours," explained Silver Birch. "Retire into the silence and learn to be still, passive. Wait, and the manifestation of the spirit can reveal itself."

"Is there any means whereby I can decide whether particular thoughts that enter my mind come from my side or yours?"

"It is all a matter of learning how to have control over the mind so that it can be still and be tuned in, so that instead of being a wanderer it can be placed under control by yourself, so that, held in perfect silence, it may respond to the higher vibrations. That is why intuition comes in a flash—because our vibration is quick and speedy and subtle. The thoughts from your world of matter are slow, they are sluggish, they are heavy."

"Does that apply to the most exalted soul on this plane at the moment?" asked the sitter.

"Yes, it applies to every soul. Remember this, you are twofold in nature. There is the ancestry of the animal and the portion of the Great Spirit constantly at war within your being, and there is yourself, you, with the free will to accomplish your evolution. You have to subdue the long line of animal that is part of your evolution and you have to learn to allow the Great Spirit that is latent to unfold itself.

"The Great Spirit is within every human being, within every facet of life, for all is the Great Spirit and the Great

Spirit is all. Within some beings the Great Spirit only stirs quietly, like the gentle zephyr. In others the Great Spirit is like the mighty raging wind. It is all a question of development. The Great Spirit has stirred within your soul and, touched by sorrow, the Great Spirit within you is striving to express itself still more. That is why you are on your quest. That is why you are here tonight. That is why you will continue to search, because your feet are now on the road that leads to spiritual truths."

"Do you mean that desire is the first step in development?" queried the sitter.

"Yes," said Silver Birch. "First comes the desire to know, in humility, in earnestness, in reverence, and with that desire the determination to use that knowledge not only for bringing certainty to yourself but to be of service to others. You desire to serve and you have striven to serve, and there are many who have upheld you for many years when your heart has been weary and your soul has grown tired in the fight and you have wondered whether it would not be best to retire from the scenes of activity and to seek in quietude those pleasures, aesthetic pleasures, that you think would bring you happiness. But the restlessness of the stirring Great Spirit within you and the inspiration from my world have encouraged you to go on with your fight to help those less fortunate than yourself."

Silver Birch told the visiting MP of the guides who were assisting him from the spirit world, and went on:

"I said that to you to make you realise the love that comes to you from our world. If all of you who sought to serve realised the great wealth of love and power that surged round you and knew how you were upheld and encouraged and enthused and sustained in all your labours, you would fight even with greater ardour and zeal and intensity. Not one effort to serve has ever been in vain. Though often misunderstood, misinterpreted and ridiculed by those who should have been

your friends and occasionally betrayed by those whom you
have trusted, your service will live on."

"What advice have you to give me?" asked the sitter.

"You do not require detailed advice," answered Silver
Birch. "You are doing greater work than you know. When
those who are engaged in service say to me, 'What can I do?'
my heart is full of joy, for it is a recognition that even as they
render service they strive to give greater service. Continue to
help the weak and the helpless, to give strength to those who
need it, light to those in darkness, a helping hand to the lame
and the struggling. Fight to abolish all cruelty, especially that
cruelty that horrifies your soul—the cruelty to mankind's
greatest friends, the world of animals."

Then Silver Birch spoke of the difficulty experienced by
guides in expressing themselves in earthly activities. "They
have to register in the world of matter," he said, "and that is
not easy, for you know the vibrations that come to us from
your world are not all that they should be. There is so much
darkness where there should be light, so much ignorance
where there should be knowledge, so much foolishness where
there should be wisdom, so much hunger where there should
be plenty, so much misery where there should be happiness,
so many hovels where there should be fit habitations for all, so
much cruelty where there should be kindness, so much hate
where there should be love. It is only through a few
instruments that the power of the spirit can express itself, but
the number is constantly increasing and the tide turns in our
favour.

"It was when sorrow came that your soul was touched,"
Silver Birch reminded the sitter.

"Do you think that that sorrow was brought for a
purpose?" the MP asked.

"From the greatest sorrow comes the greatest knowledge,"
was the reply. "All life is compensation, from shadow into

sunshine, from storm into refuge. Light and dark, storm and shine, wind and silence—these are all but reflections of the Great Spirit. The Great Spirit is in every facet of life. Because of shadow you appreciate sunshine. Because of struggle you appreciate peace. Life is enjoyed through comparisons. The soul finds its own in the bitter crucible of experience, trial and suffering and emerges purified, strengthened, touched, ready for an understanding of life's greater purpose and meaning."

"Then is suffering brought to one deliberately, for the purpose of enabling one to realise what it is necessary to have for one's unfoldment?"—"Yes, for the soul has to have all varieties of experience before it can unfold the highest. The soul is eternal and carries with it the result of every thought, of every spoken word, of every deed, and you are what you have made yourself—second by second, minute by minute, hour by hour, day by day, week by week, month by month, year by year. You achieve your own growth and all actions that you perform determine the state of your evolution. No one else accomplishes that growth for you."

"Do you differentiate between deliberate and automatic actions?" the guest next asked.

"That which is done automatically does not mean that the law of cause and effect has ceased to operate. It only stresses that it is in existence. You perform deeds because of what you are."—"Then you would say that one is what one is as a consequence of what one has done in the past on this sphere?"

"Yes, you are what you are because of what you have done and you will be what you will be because of what you are now. The law of cause and effect operates in unbroken, perfect sequence, and the law of the Great Spirit is so perfect in its operation that it never fails. Though the children of the Great Spirit may cheat the laws of state, none can evade the operations of natural law, for the soul carries with it its eternal registration of what it has accomplished and you are known for what you are, not for what you are not or what you pretend to be."

"Don't you think that all men realise when they are wrong?" asked the MP.

"No. Sometimes a man is deaf to the voice of conscience, his heart is hardened, his soul has become covered up and the life force of the Great Spirit is being choked. Men do not always realise that they are wrong. If they did, there would be no war in your world of matter, there would be no cruelty, no starvation. There would not be so much disease and there would not be an excess of plenty while others starved."

"How can one alter that?"—"By you and I and all of us being determined that the inequalities of selfish materialism shall be vanquished and the bounty of the Great Spirit made available to all His children, that disease and slums, and ill-health and poverty, and all those things which restrict the human soul and body shall be driven from the face of the world of matter, because we know that they are wrong. We must make the Great Spirit within each person so responsive that it will know what it has to do before it leaves your world of matter."

Bearing in mind that the MP—like many Spiritualists—was involved in animal welfare it is apposite to feature what the guide once said about spirit help for reformers. He told his circle:

"What we preach fits in with all the noble and elevated ideas that have come to the vision of all the reformers, all the saints, all the seers and all the idealists who have striven in every age to render service.

"Because they were great souls, their spiritual eyes caught glimpses of the life that could be, and that vision of beauty sustained them in all their adversity and struggle. They realised the spirit plan that, one day, will be put into practice, and so they strove to raise up the children of matter, to serve.

"Though they were vilified, though they were opposed and ridiculed by those they came to help, their work lived on, even as the work that is being done today in countless small temples, such as this, will live on, though many of the people will be forgotten.

"The mighty power of the Spirit has been launched once again in your world of matter, and the children of matter do not possess the power to stem that mighty tide.

"Your world thinks it solves its problems by the shedding of blood. But no problem was ever solved in that way, for bloodshed is needless and leads nowhere.

"Why cannot they use the reason which the Great Spirit has given them? Why do they think that their only solution must be to kill as many as possible, that the one who is the greatest killer is accounted the victor? It is a strange world you live in."

'Through every phase of life'

"Oh, Great White Spirit, we seek to reveal Thee as the infinite law behind every manifestation of eternal life. We realise that Thou hast been seen through distorted eyes in the days gone by. They have thought of Thee as a jealous and an angry God, a God of war.

"But we seek to reveal Thee as the infinite Spirit that pulsates through every phase of life, Who dost show Thyself in the operation of every natural law. We seek to reveal Thee as the Great Spirit of infinite wisdom and understanding, love and truth, the Great Spirit that is seen in the lives of all who seek to uplift those who are weak, those who are distressed, those who are downcast.

"Thou art not to be found, oh, Great Spirit, in any one book, in any one church, in any one mosque, in any one temple, in any one synagogue. Thine is the boundless spirit of life that cannot be restricted or limited or compressed within the finite understanding of the children of matter.

"But Thou art not so far removed from them that they cannot find Thee. Thou art within them, spirit of Thy spirit. Thou dost seek to express Thyself within every being, so that as Thy spirit rises through lives of service Thou art revealed, Thy laws are understood and the children of matter begin to learn the purpose for which Thou hast fashioned them, their relationship with one another and with Thee.

"And, in the understanding of that great truth there will come a new light in the world of matter, a new hope. Peace will reign and strife will be abolished. Selfishness will disappear, misery will be replaced by joy and all who are denied that which is necessary for their sustenance will live in a real kingdom of heaven on earth.

"This is the Great Spirit Whom we seek to reveal, Whose laws we strive to teach, so that in understanding these truths of the Spirit Thy children of matter may live lives that are straight and upright, they may cast away their bondage, cease to be servile, that they may learn not to approach Thee on bended knees, cringing for divine favours, but to claim their heritage—the right to express Thee in their daily lives."

Chapter Three

'WE WILL NOT FAIL YOU'

A FEW months after Silver Birch helped a Congregational minister to arrive at the truth concerning what awaits all at death, the guide assisted him to return from the Other Side to comfort his wife. For soon after his first visit, the Rev J. Penry Davey, a senior Army chaplain, passed into the Higher Life.

Mr Davey was invited to meet the guide by Hannen Swaffer. In brilliant style, Silver Birch gave the minister advice applicable to all.

"Do not accept everything that is told you," he said. "Use your own reason to test, to challenge all that we say and all that will be said to you, all that you will hear. If aught that we tell you offends your reason, reject it. We make no claim to infallibility. We only say that we can give you those truths which have been known to the saints and the seers for centuries, that have been forgotten or buried beneath the debris of theology and creed. We strive to rescue those ancient, eternal truths which point the way to man's regeneration, to his spiritual freedom, his economic and social liberation.

"No man can serve two masters. You know that. Search yourself, search your own heart, your own being; and there you will find the answer to many, indeed to all your problems. What is true in the beliefs that you have held will endure. Nothing can shake them. What is false must be discarded. Hoary error must give way when confronted with divine inspiration.

"We do not yield one inch in our implacable opposition to all which has held your world in bondage for too long. We are opposed to the structure of creeds and dogma and ritual that has been built in the name of religion. What is false must be discarded; what is of God will endure. The vapourings worshipped by man for too long, the dogmas that emanate not from inspiration or revelation but from motives, often political, do not win our support.

"For years you have sought to give service, thinking not of yourself but only of others, until you have worn yourself weary in the task of trying to do good," said the spirit guide to the minister at the commencement of the seance. "That, perhaps, you will deny, but your wife will agree with me."

"I do," said the minister's wife, who accompanied her husband.

"Your work has not always been in places where the fierce light of publicity has shone upon you," went on the guide, "although that has happened once or twice. Rather have you sought to do what good you can wherever you can. And now that your eyes have been opened at last—when you think it is rather late and wish that this knowledge had come earlier—you wonder what service you can still render to your fellows."

"That is true," remarked the minister.

"You know, you can only receive truth when you are ready to receive truth, not before," said Silver Birch. "Truth comes when the mind is inclined to its reception, for when truth feels that she will get a chilly reception when she knocks at your door, and will fail to gain admittance, truth stays away until she knows the doorway is open and you are ready to receive her."

Invited to ask questions of the guide, the minister said he hardly knew what to ask. There were so many things strange to him and some rather difficult. "Put to me the most difficult, and if I can help you I will," said the guide. The

minister wondered whether he was wise in giving up the work
he had been doing and asked whether he would receive the
necessary help to fit himself for something quite different.

"How many times have you yourself expounded, 'Seek and
ye shall find . . . Ask and ye shall receive . . . Knock and it
shall be opened unto you'?" asked Silver Birch.

"A good many times," answered the minister.

"I say it now to you," said the guide. "But I say it with the
conviction of knowledge, for I know that in my world there
waits an army of ministers of the Great Spirit, ready to serve
your world, waiting for instruments like you to say to us, 'I
am ready; use me.' We will not fail you, but you have to make
the first move. You have to show that you are prepared to
follow truth wherever she will lead you. You are leaving
behind the old foundations, but you are not wandering forth
into the desert, you are not going out into the wilderness, for
you have moved out of uncertainty into spiritual verities.

"This is the power of the spirit, of which you have talked
so much and yet have failed to understand. This is the descent
of the Holy Ghost, as you have called it. This is the means by
which the Great Spirit sheds His knowledge, His wisdom,
His truth, His revelation, His love to your world. We are but
instruments, who have qualified by long years of service,
evolution, growth, experience, to help your world. We ask
nothing for ourselves; only that we may have the privilege of
giving you all that we possess so that you may use it to help
others. Perhaps I can help you to clarify some of your own
problems."

"Thank you," said the minister, not knowing of Silver
Birch's insistence that he shall never be thanked.

"Do not thank me," said the guide. "Thank the Great
Spirit, Whom we all try to serve. We are only instruments;
thank the One Whom we strive to represent. For many years
we were voices in the wilderness, crying out, preparing the

way. We strove to make your world listen, but it was deaf. It would not hear the voice of the spirit. More than thrice did we call before we found our Samuels."

The guide was then asked to tell the minister what he knew of Jesus.

"I have seen the Nazarene many times," Silver Birch said. "He does not sit on the right hand of the Father, and the Father is not on a golden throne. The Nazarene is a great and evolved spirit. He is not so far away, magnified and deified beyond the reach of your world. He is close at hand, directing this truth that you call Spiritualism but which to us is merely the operation of natural laws.

"It is he who directs these efforts, who strives to inspire all those who minister to your world so that they shall continue to heal the afflicted, to comfort the mourner, to give light to those who are ignorant, to teach those who do not know where to turn, to provide a shelter for the many wanderers, to give courage to those who are tired in mind and body. It is he, the real being whom we have seen and who encourages us in our mission to your world. Where did you think he was?"

"If I had thought about it, I would have said that he is on the right hand of the Father, and I have thought of the Father more as a being," confessed the minister. "But now I have a different view of God."

"Yes," said Silver Birch. "The Law has no right hand, it has no left hand, for it is the Law, perfect in its operation, never failing, never making mistakes, enduring for all time, without beginning and without end. Forget those old ideas of a personal deity—they must go—and think of the Great Spirit as the Law behind all life. And think of the Nazarene as one like yourself, who has evolved much higher but not so high that you cannot touch him, not beyond your reach, for the road he has trod you are treading, the powers he had unfolded you can unfold.

"Whatever he did, you can do. 'And greater things than these shall ye do . . .' 'Behold I send you a comforter, the spirit of truth.' That is what you are hearing now. I do not mean that I am the Comforter, that I am the spirit of truth. But I am part of that power which comes from the Great Spirit, which is directed by the Nazarene, so that your world shall understand and get rid of all those foul blots on your civilisation."

The guide told the sitter that once contact with the spirit world is made it always remains. "Once the magnetic link is forged, it cannot be broken," he said, "for once you are accessible to the power of the spirit and you have enabled yourself to be touched by its power, that tie can never be dissolved and you are always susceptible to these things.

"Usually it is through sorrow that the touch is first made—the sorrow of bereavement, the sorrow of pain and illness, or sadness. That is the part that pain plays in your earthly life."

Silver Birch explained that on the Other Side they had to choose their gifts, just as earthly instruments could sometimes choose their psychic gifts—and he had chosen teaching. "We choose, as you can choose, those that can best be developed," he said. "If one lies nearer the surface, that is the most easy for development. Sometimes you have two or three gifts which can be called from the well of your being, and you are asked to choose."

Answering another question the guide said: "I teach principles founded on spiritual truth. If those were applied to all your problems, they would soon disappear. I am not impervious to the cry of suffering. I would that I could put the whole load on my own shoulders, bear all the burden on my own back. Your world must pay the price; justice will be done. You have to spread knowledge, for only armed with the knowledge can humanity find that peace which is waiting for it. Try and see in all the suffering a lesson to be learned and know that even though your world seems full of despair the will of the Great Spirit is being done and there is no power on earth that can thwart that mighty purpose. It can delay it, and obscure it for a little while, but a new world is born and these are the signs that the old is crumbling. The signs of transformation are being witnessed by you.

"You have not much longer to wait before those who think they rule the world will find their despotism and their tyranny is ended. But remember, the Great Spirit did not put them there; you put them there. They were born of hatred and ignorance and a condition that the people of your world made. The Great Spirit has been more than generous with the bounty that is provided in your world. There is enough for all. There is no need to fight over land, which belongs to no people, no nation, for it belongs to the Great Spirit. You are all merely His tenants, who sojourn in your world for a while.

"You can solve all your problems once you have knowledge without spilling one drop of blood, without cutting off one life. But ignorance and vested interest have been the barriers. And every time one like yourself enrolls in the army of those who fight against materialism, so the forces of darkness are pushed one stage further back. We cannot work miracles. We are not spiritual 'medicine men.' We are expounding a Law, because we know its operation. We have laboured for long and are beginning to see the fruits of our labours. We are not filled with despair, we are confident.

"With the breath of my being I serve you always. Go forward. Put behind you all thoughts of fear and know that love comes to you; the love of those who are bound to you by ties of blood and who are separated only by the thin veil of matter but who are close to you in spirit and who are with you, seeking always to guide you; and the love of many who are one with you in spirit, whom you do not know but who know you and who have waited for you both from the time of your birth.

"They have inspired you, guarded and guided you and exerted an unseen but real influence in your lives. They have enjoyed all your happiness and have shared your sorrows, and have been with you in times of laughter and tears. They are at one with you and will not fail you. As you make one step nearer to them, so they will help you always to take the next step in front of you. Do not hesitate; go forward. Do not be dismayed if many whom you try to help spurn your aid. That does not matter. Do not worry if they say you are mad. You know, they said of old that the disciples were drunk. May the Great Spirit bless you both."

Then, within four months, the minister's wife came again. She and her husband were still together, but on opposite sides of the veil. The guide greeted her: "It is a joy to have you here and to see that you have borne all with such fortitude and with such strength, for you have, indeed, passed through a great test. Still your knowledge has stood firm and you have not faltered. Your husband is a great soul and he is with you, so anxious, so full of love, to reach you."

"Yes, I know he is," replied the sitter.

"He says that he has revealed himself many times, but at other times he is sorry that he has caused a little confusion in his anxiety to demonstrate his nearness to you."

"Yes," said the wife, who had been receiving messages from her "dead" husband at her own home circle.

"You will see how, almost unseen, he has been 'pulling strings' all the time, for he only has your happiness and your welfare at stake," went on the guide, referring to the sitter's problems. "His work is not over; neither is yours, for you too, like him, have much in front of you. Be patient. It has taken him a long time to get accustomed to his new environment, but he has made rapid strides. He is very anxious that you continue with your circle."

"Yes, I am doing so," said the minister's wife.

"He says that when you get passive, quiet, settled, he can show himself to you. You have seen him?"—"Yes, I think so."

"But it is too indefinite? You look and then he is not there, but he was before."—"I told him it was not a very good likeness of him," said the wife.

"Yes, but practice will make perfect," promised the guide. "Do not grieve, even inside yourself. He has been promoted. He has earned his promotion. Long years of service have been rewarded and he has moved on, but not away from you. He will be with you always, for there is no one that matters to him like you do. You know that.

"And you have the greatest power in the whole universe, the power of love. That has brought you together and will see that you are never parted. You have knowledge and if sometimes you cannot see all the way be grateful that knowledge has been vouchsafed to you so that you can build on a foundation not of hope, not of guesswork or speculation, but of fact that will remain unshaken no matter what wind of circumstances will blow."

Asked whether she had any question to ask, the sitter said she was a little puzzled by the sudden and unexpected passing. She wondered what determined the time of "death."

"When the spirit is ready, it leaves," answered the guide. "When the apple is ripe, it drops from the tree. Sometimes the tree is shaken and the apples drop before they are ripe; then they are not good to eat. Sometimes the spirit is forced to leave the body before it is ripe, and it is not ready. But in the case of your husband the spirit was ready, the body had served its purpose and so it dropped away. You could not have delayed it; neither could he. One day the same thing will happen to all of you. Do not fear it."

Then the sitter told of a message her husband had given her which had not yet materialised.

"Time is very difficult to judge," said Silver Birch, "because we can see results, and sometimes it is not possible to gauge the time it will take for the result to materialise in your world. Some are better at this calculation than others. But there is no need for you to have any anxiety. He will reveal himself again and again and again, and guide you and cherish you. Try to go on and give this knowledge to others, for even as he has helped you so it will help them."

"That's my great desire," said the woman, who was able to think of comforting others even within a few weeks of her own great bereavement.

"You will," promised the guide. "Try to lighten the load, try to point the way, try to illumine the darkness of others. There is so much sorrow, so much sadness, so much misery that need not be. All the love of our world seeks to express itself through instruments who can spread its power so that humanity, which has lost its way, can find that path which leads to peace and understanding and help to abolish all the inequalities and cruelties that are blots on this world of yours.

"Your garden of Eden is here. Your Paradise is in front of you. Only man's greed, stupidity, selfishness and cruelty stand in the way. It could all be attained in a day. There is so much work to be done. We need all who are willing to be instruments of that Great Power that fashioned all life and seeks to teach it how to live. May the Great Spirit bless you. When you go, your husband goes with you. Love goes to its own."

'We thank Thee for the humble'

"Oh, Great White Spirit, we thank Thee for the gift of life. We thank Thee because Thou hast merged Thy spirit into us and enabled us to partake in Thy infinite purpose, helping to manifest Thee, to reveal Thy love, Thy wisdom, Thy truth and Thy knowledge.

"Oh, Great Spirit, we raise our voices in thanksgiving for all the manifold expressions of Thee which are revealed to us in every living phase of the universe. We thank Thee for the opportunity of returning across the gulf of 'death,' over the bridge of love.

"We thank Thee for all the willing service that is rendered to Thee and Thy children, whether they dwell in bodies of matter or whether they express themselves in the realms of spirit.

"We thank Thee for all those who reveal Thy divinity in their lives and who, because of that, enable their idealism, their nobility and their sacrifice to be an inspiration to others less evolved than they are.

"We thank Thee for all the revelations of Thee and Thy infinite purpose given to Thy children throughout every age. We thank Thee for all the acts of martyrdom, of heroism, for all the pioneers and reformers, all who have sought and striven to uplift those amongst whom they dwelt.

"We thank Thee for those who have sought to reveal Thy inspiration and to make Mankind understand the laws of the Spirit. We thank Thee for all those who, because they lived in the world of matter, have been enabled to confer a boon upon their fellows.

"We thank Thee for all the channels between the world of matter and the world of spirit, many unconscious, but all of whom make it possible for a fuller understanding of the great purpose of eternal life to be made manifest.

"We thank Thee for the humble and the contrite hearts who seek Thee on diverse pathways, sometimes in differing churches and temples, and sometimes professing no religion, but only seeking to express the highest that is within them.

"We thank Thee, oh, Great White Spirit, for the opportunity given to us to render service to Thee by serving those whom we love and who aid us to spread knowledge and truth and teach Thy children of matter how to liberate themselves from spiritual bondage and become free.

"May all that is done in this temple and other temples speed the day when all Mankind, because of their greater knowledge, will dwell in amity, concord and peace and exhibit in their lives that love which comes from Thee, the great infinite love of the Great Eternal Spirit.

"That is the prayer of Thy Indian servant, who seeks to serve, and may the prayer be translated speedily into actuality."

Chapter Four

'ALL TRUTH IS WONDERFUL'

APART from a short break in the summer, in latter years the Hannen Swaffer Home Circle met monthly. The guide's medium, Maurice Barbanell, would drive home after a day's work at "Psychic News"—he was the paper's founder and editor—greet guests invited to attend and settle comfortably in a settee whilst those present chatted quietly until Silver Birch manifested.

So it was that for many decades Silver Birch imparted his words of wisdom in a small flat in a pleasant part of London whilst buses and taxis took weary workers home. For unknown to them and those walking in the tree-lined street outside one whom the world regards as dead offered wise counsel as the Seen and Unseen temporarily merged.

"To you, this is a little room," said Silver Birch. "To us, it is a grand temple. These little walls have vanished. There is radiance, illumination dazzling in its brilliance. Hundreds upon hundreds are assembled here, each with a mission to perform; some to serve, some to be served.

"That vast concourse belongs to all peoples and nations, to the present and to the past. There are prophets, seers, sages, wise men of the East and the West, of high and low estate, philosophers of Greece and Rome, Syria, Chaldea, Persia and Babylon, mingled with those of later generations from Italy, France and Germany. They exchange their knowledge and focus it all so that it shall be at your service.

"That is only one fragment of what is happening. There are your own, those you know and the many whom you do not know in your material consciousness but whom you do know in that larger consciousness in which you dwell for fleeting moments."

Earlier in the sitting, after Silver Birch had given some information regarding healing, one of the sitters remarked, "That is a wonderful truth."

"All truth is wonderful," replied the guide. "It is error that is so foolish. And yet there are so many who would rather cling to error, because they are familiar with error, even though they know it is error, rather than seek the strange landmarks of wonderful truth.

"They would rather be weak when they could be strong; they would rather dwell ,in darkness with undisturbed faith built on error than seek the light. The path of the truth-seeker is not an easy one, for the pioneer does not achieve truth with ease.

"The things that are most valuable and most highly prized are not lightly earned, but only through perplexity and doubt, with earnestness, with reverence, with the desire to know as your motto, can you achieve those truths which mean so much.

"But always remember this also. The soul must be prepared. No truth comes to you until the soul has earned that truth. Till then, your efforts are in vain, for you are not ready and equipped. That is what was meant by casting pearls before swine."

Then a sitter mentioned an effort to revise the Bible that seemed foredoomed to failure.

"Let them try," said the guide. "Encourage all those who are on the side of opposing vested interest. Let this new spirit of reform permeate where it can.

"Not all is achieved in a blinding flash of revelation. Some-times another method has to be employed—the little drops of water that drip away on the stone until they wear it away.

"Ours is a great task. We do not seek to perform wonders

that will enable ignorance to stare at us with mouth agape and with wide-eyed astonishment. We do not seek to convert masses in one instantaneous revelation.

"Ours is the constant fight against selfishness, self-interest, the powers that belong to all the darkness of life. Prejudice, superstition, error, jealousy, greed, avarice, hate—against these we are at war.

"We seek to advance our cause wherever we can, wherever we find receptive hearts, receptive minds, receptive souls.

"For years it was with difficulty that we laboured. The opposition seemed so gigantic, the obstacles insuperable, yet we toiled on unceasingly, knowing always that with the power of the Great Spirit behind us and with a few faithful, valiant hearts to co-operate with us, we could not fail.

"You who live today can see the fruits of nearly a century of arduous toil. All this is as naught compared with what shall be achieved, for the tide has turned. Now we are marching forward to victory and nothing can stop us . . .

"Just as calmly, yet as emphatically, do we declare we are marching forward to victory. Light triumphs over darkness, knowledge defeats ignorance, joy replaces sorrow and truth is the victor."

Then, obviously addressing Spiritualists the world over, the guide said:

"I want you who are engaged in this task to know always that the power behind you desires to serve you as you serve others.

"How I wish that the blinkers were removed from your eyes, so that you could see. How I wish that you could know as I know.

"You would never despair. Gloom would find not even a tarrying place in your beings, for you would realise the strength that surrounds you."

Giving a hint of the system used on the Other Side to communicate inspiration from the higher planes, Silver Birch explained that "ours is an ascending ladder.

"Each rung is joined to the one above," he went on, "so that the lowliest in your world of matter has access to the highest in the realm of spirit.

"The ladder of Jacob was not a figment of the imagination, but the symbol of an eternal reality, for up that ladder every soul can climb, rung by rung. From earth to heaven it ranges, supported always by the power of the Great Spirit."

The guide devoted this particular sitting to conversation more personal to the sitters than was his usual custom. He had been discussing difficulties before he uttered the following benediction which is applicable to all:

"When shadows cross your path, remember they are but shadows, not reality. When clouds obscure the sun, remember they are but clouds. When beset by trial and difficulty, remember these are but birds of passage that will continue their flight when they have but rested for a short while.

"The knowledge that you all possess is more priceless than all the treasures of the world of matter. We do not bring you gold or silver, diamonds or precious jewels. Rather do we seek to bring the priceless jewels of the spirit, the greatest treasures that you can have.

"Prize them. Put them in a setting of love and realise that these are the gifts that the Great Spirit bestows on you with loving care and divine affection.

"Look up always, not down. Realise that the mighty and majestic power which brought you into being and breathed into you the life-giving essence of its own spirit will uphold and sustain you day by day.

"Incline your hearts to His, subdue your souls to His, fill your minds with the wisdom that comes from His inexhaustible reservoir and know that those who seek to give service and labour for the upliftment of the weak, the fallen and the needy are protected by the mantle of the spirit.

"Go forward, steady and sure in the knowledge which is yours. Use it wisely and well. Remember your responsibilities as instruments of the Great Spirit, who in our many ways we all seek to serve, so as to hear His benediction, 'Well done, good and faithful servant.' May the Great Spirit bless you all."

The guide assured those in attendance, "You will all live after you have 'died,' and you will not realise until then what it is to live or to feel the real glory of life untrammelled, free to rejoice in liberty of spirit which your imprisoned souls cannot understand today.

"How can a bird which has never been outside the cage realise what it is to fly from branch to branch, to have no prison bars?"

"Why was the soul imprisoned in the body at all?" asked one of the sitters.

"Just as the seed is put into darkness, there to gain strength before it can burst into life, the seed of human life is put into darkness to obtain the strength of human experience before it can burst into the life of the spirit," was the reply.

"All the experiences of human life are part of the great scheme. Those experiences which you like least of all—the sadness, the bitterness, the tears, the disappointments, the suffering and the pain—these are very valuable for your souls.

"But you cannot realise that at the time. It is only when you can look back on the whole, and not judge by the part, that you can get a clear picture of the values of life. Through all your adversities the character is tried. Through tears and sorrow the soul is strengthened.

"We look at life not through physical eyes but with the knowledge of spirit life, where the true balance is struck. Those who live wisely are the ones who seek to turn all experiences into advantage to their souls, who do not try to flee from trial and temptation but seek to use the innermost strength to face difficulties, for it is in that spirit that character is evolved and strengthened. How very simple are these great truths, so simple that they are beyond many of your intellectuals."

Commenting on the fact that the circle was then composed mostly of young people, Silver Birch said, "I rejoice that, whilst you have so many years of physical life in front of you, you are enabled to appreciate the realities of spiritual truth."

"We regard it as a great privilege," remarked one of the regular sitters.

"And as a responsibility," said the guide. "That is the price of all knowledge. You all have the greatest privilege in the world of matter, the privilege of being able to use your knowledge for service. When all the things that are counted great in your world of matter have passed away, the service that you have rendered to one another will yield your eternal progress.

"We preach the religion of service, service, service, not of creeds, not of rituals, not of doctrines—unless they make you serve. Ceremony, observances, these are unimportant. What does count is that you exercise your spirit—the Great Spirit that is within you."

"What is your definition of religion?" asked another circle member.

"To me, it means but one thing," said Silver Birch. "To serve the Great Spirit by serving His children."

This guide then told how, in the production of psychic phenomena, use was made of all the materials in the room as well as of the psychic powers of the sitters.

"Do you mean that you extract substances from them?" he was asked.

"Yes, we make use of the carpet, the curtains, books, even of the furniture," he replied. "We who are not encased in matter have to use matter, and we obtain it to some extent from the actual substances that are here. We take a little from everything so as not to destroy things. Otherwise, you would find your furniture falling to pieces."

"Is that why sometimes in materialisation seances the curtains, say, wear out quickly?" someone asked.

"Yes, that is the reason," said the guide. "But we are very careful."

Replying to another question, Silver Birch said that sometimes colour was taken from material things in order to provide the colours used in materialisations.

"When you know more about our work," he said, "you will learn that nothing is wasted. But the greatest power of all is the power that comes from within each one of you. That is the greatest ingredient."

This guide gave the complete answer to those who criticise Spiritualists for "disturbing the dead" and, they say, "dragging them back unwillingly to talk to us."

"I cannot make you realise the pleasure it gives me to be able to talk with you through this medium," he said. "To be with you in the spirit is no new experience for me, but to talk with you face to face makes me very happy. Always remember, I am here to serve you. I am your friend, unseen perhaps, but your willing servant. If at any time I can be of service, you call on me. You disturb the dead!"

One sitter asked about an experience that had befallen a relative of hers. He wondered whether it was an influence that was good or evil.

"You can all banish from your minds the thought that anything that is unenlightened—or, as you would say, evil—can ever touch you," the guide said. "You live and move under the protection of the Great Spirit and His laws.

"If there is no evil in your hearts, then only good can reach you, for only good can dwell where goodness reigns. None but the servants of the Great Spirit come into your presence. You need have no fears. The power which envelops you, the power which supports and seeks to guide you and inspire you is the power that emanates from the Great Spirit of all.

"That power can sustain you in all your trials and difficulties. That power can change your storms into sunshine, and bring you out of the darkness of despair into the light of knowledge. Your feet are set on pathways of progress. There is no need for fear . . .

"Much that is regarded as important in your world is but a veneer that has only a passing value.

"True education is the growth of the soul," continued the guide. "You become educated as your soul-powers reach out and unfold their latent divinity.

"The mere acquisition of knowledge is of little value, and might be a very selfish pursuit unless the knowledge is acquired to be of service to others.

"Do not judge by the outer semblance. The difference between us always is that you judge from the outer manifestation while we who see with the eyes of the spirit see motive and purpose, which are more important. Strive to see the eternal realities behind the passing phases.

"Rank, title, profession or calling, the colour of skins—what are these in the sight of the Great Spirit? True wealth and true nobility are of the soul, the spirit, the mind, for these are the eternal realities.

"The Nazarene taught the same things: 'The kingdom of heaven is within'; 'Lay not up for yourself treasures on earth where moth and rust doth corrupt.' We teach the same truth for truth is truth and eternal principles cannot change.

"I know it is hard for you who are encased in matter to think in terms of spiritual reality, but that is the purpose of our return, to try and help you to adjust yourselves to get the true focus and perspective of life.

"Remember that your world is but an infinitesimal fragment of your eternal lives. Do not confuse the shadows with the reality."

Silver Birch reminded the circle that, though they had grown accustomed to the teachings that he brought, to others —some of them very weary, some of them sick at heart, some of them perplexed and full of doubt—the spirit message came as "a breath of sweet, fresh, clean air that blows away the lingering cobwebs and enables the mind to become invigorated.

"Sometimes the soul has to travel through much perplexity and doubt, through much sadness, weariness and disillusionment before it is ready for the light of spiritual truth," he continued.

"Our work is spreading—that much I know and can say with certainty. That is why I always stress the note of optimism and tell you we are marching forward to victory."

'In every phase of life'

"Oh, Great White Spirit, how shall we explain Thy infinitude to those whose minds are encased in matter? How shall we explain Thee, Who art beyond explanation, Thou Who cannot be measured, Whose wisdom surpasses the wisdom of the highest that is known, Whose love exceeds all that which has been expressed?

"How shall we express Thee, the Great White Spirit of all life, Whose spirit pulsates through every manifestation of being, Who art seen in every phase of life, whether it be the life that is known to the world of matter or the life that is revealed in the realm of spirit?

"We point to the universe and all that it contains, to the rhythm of life as it expresses itself in every motion. We point to the rising and the setting sun, to the glittering stars in the firmament, to the pattering rain drops, to the ebb and flow of the mighty ocean, to the ripple of the murmuring stream, to the drone of the bee, to the nodding of the flower, to the roar of the thunder and the flash of the lightning.

"We point to every manifestation of life and declare that they are expressions of Thee and Thy infinite law, for Thou art law and dost reveal Thyself in immutable, unchangeable, eternal law.

"We who belong to the higher manifestations of life return to demonstrate the unbroken sequence of natural law as it is known in the world of spirit. We seek to reveal Thee as Thou art, to demonstrate the superiority of the spirit, to reveal the kinship of the spirit that unites us with Thee, and to make the children of matter realise that they are a part of Thee and Thy spirit broods within them all, ever seeking to find expression.

"Oh, Great White Spirit, we pay tribute to Thee for allowing our higher selves to rise to the surface to seek harmony with Thee, the oversoul of life. We are reaching out and clasping that which is our divine heritage and finding the reality which is within the depths of every soul.

"We pray that in this temple of light we may be enabled to demonstrate some of the laws of the spirit, neglected throughout the centuries but revealed to the few who have sought Thee.

"This is the prayer of Thy Indian servant, who seeks only to serve and thus demonstrate the law of love."

Chapter Five

'YOU ARE THE GREAT SPIRIT'

"THE magnitude of spiritual truth has brought you all together, and you have conferred one with another to try to find a new strength and new courage, to return to your own lands with a new understanding and a new hope."

Silver Birch used these words one September Sunday night in a message to delegates who had attended meetings of the International Spiritualist Congress, and who had been invited, with a few others, to a special seance.

"Your world of matter cannot be silent to the voice of the Spirit any longer, for you stand at the crossroads and a choice has to be made," continued Silver Birch.

"Your Churches have failed you; they are bankrupt. Your men of science have failed you; they seek to destroy instead of building. Your philosophers have failed you; theirs is but the empty talk of idle speculation. Your statesmen have failed you; they have not learned the supreme lesson that only through sacrifice can peace come to your world.

"In his despair, the child of the Great Spirit cries out for guidance.

"We remind you of the great trust that is reposed in you, the great responsibility that is yours to bear, for there is One that cannot fail—the Great Spirit of all life.

"If you will but allow His power to guide you, His wisdom to lead you, His love to sustain you, you will find the solution of all your troubles, for you will all find your selves, the true selves, the greater selves that seek not for glory for themselves alone but only desire to serve.

"Your world is full of strife and bitterness, full of discord. It is full of tears and misery and bloodshed. And yet each cries, 'Give us peace.'

"I urge you all to remember the potentiality that lies within yourselves. *You* are the Great Spirit, each one of you. His infinite power is latent within you, if you will but call it into being and let it rise to the surface and break all the bonds of limitation that stand in the way.

"Reveal yourselves in the fullness of its hidden glory. Realise that you are indeed the Great Spirit, with infinite power at your disposal, and you will indeed be the instruments of the new age, which slowly is beginning to dawn over a darkened world.

"Put not your faith in the world of matter or in those who dwell in that world, no matter how high a place they occupy. Look beyond! Try to catch that inspiration that ever seeks to illumine your lives with its desire to serve.

"Go forward! And, though you will find many disappointments and many failures, we will always stand behind you, seeking to enthuse you in your days of difficulty, seeking to give you hope and strength when you are tired, seeking to raise you up when you are cast down. You will never be alone. The Great Spirit will send His ministers to guard you.

"Some of you will go to far-off places. But the power of the Spirit will not disperse. It will go with you, striving always to reveal itself in your lives as you desire to serve.

"May the blessing of the Great Spirit go with each one of you, and may you realise how infinite is the love which seeks to hold you in its embrace. May you realise that you are enveloped in the mantle of divine love. May you look beyond the difficulties and the trials and the troubles of the world of matter and raise your faces to the sun, the golden symbol of the Great Spirit.

"Fill your hearts with love, your minds with knowledge, your spirits with a determination to serve. Then the will of the Great Spirit will make itself known through you, and all your hearts will beat in unison with His great heart, and you will be at one with Him."

On a different occasion when discussing the work that those convinced of Spiritualism should do, the spirit sage commented:

"We are all servants of the Great Spirit—you and I and those who work with us—seeking to do His will. We are misunderstood, often our friends are our greatest enemies. But we do our work and, because we do that which is right in the sight of the Great Spirit, we call to our aid all those forces which belong to the spirit which are stronger than your world of matter.

"And gradually good triumphs over evil, justice triumphs over injustice, and right triumphs over wrong. Sometimes the forces of your world push us back for a while, but not for ever.

"We must succeed, for we seek to save mankind from himself, to point to him those higher and better ways which will enable him to live his life in service, so that he may receive the richness of soul, spirit and mind, the peace and the happiness which do not belong to the world of matter but to the higher and greater things of the spirit."

"How is the world to be converted to the truths of Spiritualism?" a sitter asked.

"The world will not be converted in a blinding flash like Saul on the road to Damascus. Gradually, the light of spiritual truths will break through, as more people become aware of the great knowledge and more instruments are available for the power of the Great White Spirit to use.

"You must remember that the things of the Spirit require careful nurture and progress. Sudden conversions would not be enduring, and our work is intended to be permanent.

"Each soul that becomes an instrument for the Great Spirit, each soul that moves out of darkness into the light, out of ignorance into knowledge, out of superstition into truth, is helping to advance the world, for each one of these is a nail that is driven into the coffin of the world's materialism.

"What you must all learn is that there are two forms of development. You can unfold that which is of the soul and you can unfold that which is of the spirit. One is the development of only the psychic faculty, and the other is soul growth.

"Where you get the development of the psychic without the spiritual, there you have a low plane of vibration. When you get a combination of both, then you have not only a great medium, but a great man or woman."

Then there was the time when Silver Birch went on to emphasise the growing importance of the work of Spiritualism.

"The work that we do here becomes more and more necessary," he said. "In its blindness, your world will not live according to the laws of the Great Spirit. It has chosen the path that leads to darkness and to despair.

"We offer the knowledge that leads to hope, to light, to peace and to harmony. Your world may despise us, in its ignorance. It may reject the message that we bring. It may deny the power that accompanies us. But our great truth must prevail, for it is of the Great Spirit.

"Those who strive to live against the law reap for themselves the results of a bitter harvest. Those who live with the law reap a harvest of happiness and plenty in the things of matter and in the things of the Spirit.

"Through all the darkness that prevails, do not abandon hope, but be assured in the knowledge that those who work with you for the upliftment of humankind, who strive to bring better conditions into your world of matter, will prevail, for the power that is on their side is the mightiest power in the universe.

"You will not achieve that which is worth achieving without travail, without sorrow. Your world must learn its lessons in the only way it can learn them.

"We are breaking through all over the world of matter. Our message illumines minds in every part of your world, and, as the light of the Spirit breaks in on your world, so its rays disperse the darkness of your materialism."

Spiritualism, however, would be but an empty husk without mediums, those gifted men and women who through their psychic faculties are able to bridge the two worlds.

"Give us more mediums," Silver Birch urged. "We cannot have too many instruments. We are making great progress on all sides. Our forces march forward to victory.

"And remember," he continued, "that it is not only a victory for our truths, but it is also an advance in all that which is a natural corollary of the advance of spiritual truths, of the movements that are on the side of freedom, reform, amelioration, betterment, justice, progress.

"For as our power permeates your world, it permeates not only in the direction of religion, but in all fields of your human activity. And it brings a new inspiration, a new urge, a new zest, a new zeal and a new ardour to pioneers all over your world and they strive with renewed vigour to take up their tasks and to continue the fights.

"As the power of the spirit fills their beings and envelops them, all the forces that belong to the darkness of reaction inevitably retreat. Then progress is made and new pages are written in the history of humanity. All who labour with the desire to serve are helping to write those pages in letters of fire.

"Vested interest, which has been entrenched for generations, is finding itself being torn up at the roots, for its foundations were built on shifting sands and cannot endure the continuous onslaughts of truth.

"Orthodoxy in all fields is dying, and the new 'heresies' are gradually winning their way. Men see that what was considered 'heretical' is merely truth appearing in the guise of strangeness because they were unfamiliar with it."

Silver Birch reminded the circle that he forecast all this a long time ago, when he spoke of a great effort being made from the spirit world to seek out instruments in all countries. It was then, he said, that this mighty initiative was directed.

"But remember, without you we are powerless," he said. "You provide the arms with which we work. We have no hands but yours; we have no instruments but those whom you place at our disposal.

"You cannot give us too many instruments, for as soon as one is ready there are waiting all the time many in our world to use him.

"We are waiting for you; you are not waiting for us. The power which is ready to descend is infinite in its expression, multitudinous in its variety and its fashions, and shapes itself to the channels placed at its disposal.

"The great cry is—give us more and more instruments, men and women of courage, earnestness and sincerity who are prepared to forget self, to make sacrifices so that the power of the spirit shall descend in all its fullness and make life worth living in all its richness, beauty and splendour, as the Great Spirit would have it.

"Ours is an inspiring task, one that fills us with pride in the dignity of the labour we seek to do."

The guide commented again on the progress made by Spiritualism.

"We do not belong to the despised handful of yesterday," he said. "We do not belong to the shame-faced few who hid in corners. Ours is the proud array of those who know that truth is with them because they have proved it to be true, and unashamed they take their places in life, proudly proclaiming the gospel of spiritual realities.

"No longer are you derided because you espouse spiritual truths. That belongs to the ignorant yesterday. Today you are respected."

Here it is germane to highlight Silver Birch's reply to the then Archbishop of Canterbury who, on radio, called for a return to organised religion.

"Real religion is service to the Great Spirit by serving His children," said the guide. "To do that, you require no churches, no priests, no clergymen, no sacred books—unless they implant in your heart the desire to serve, and make you love the children of the Great Spirit more than you loved them before. Serve whenever you can. Help to lift your brother's load. That is religion.

"I only repeat the simple truth that many of you know, either instinctively or else through reason and logic. I bring the truths which I have learned in the larger realm of the Spirit, where all people have to face reality, where cause and effect can be seen in their immediate operation, where only those who serve are counted as higher than those who do not.

"All the pretence and shams of your world are stripped away and the soul is revealed in all its nakedness, so that its strength and its weakness can be known to all.

"I come from a world where values are known, where falsity does not exist and inequality does not reign. There are no poor and no rich in my world, except those who are poor or rich in spirit. There are no mighty and no weak, except those whose souls are mighty or weak.

"When all the things that your world of matter praises highly have faded away into the dust of the forgotten past, the eternal realities of the Spirit will endure for ever."

Then Silver Birch gave his own plea for a return to religion, not the religion of outworn creeds and elaborate ceremony, but the religion of service. He declared:

"The chief message I want to give you all is to remind you

that, as you stand at the dawn of a new year, it can provide opportunities for great service. Look around your world of matter, see the misery and the despair, the sorrow and the anguish, the many tear-stained faces. Look around and realise that there is a vast field for service. Ignorance still reigns, misused power still prevails, prejudice has still to be overcome.

"See the hunger and the starvation, those who 'suffer' because they have too much and those who suffer because they have nothing. See the many physical bodies racked with pain, unable to express as they should the power of the Great Spirit within them. See the condition of poverty and distress, the hovels that should shame all those who regard themselves as Christians.

"And remember that your world can be a Kingdom of Heaven, that it is filled potentially with all that can transform it into a garden of peace and plenty, but it is choked by the weeds of selfishness.

"We call all of you to service, asking you to forget yourselves and your own desires, to allow that which is divine to triumph over that which is earthly, so that each one of you becomes a messenger for the Great Spirit of Life.

"Each one of you should seek to carry on the work of reform, to bring cheer and happiness to all who need it, to wipe away all tears and to replace them with laughter, to fight all ignorance and superstition, to let knowledge reign in their place, to abolish all the darkness and to allow the light of divine truth to penetrate, to banish all fear, all mourning, all disease, so that love can rule triumphant."

Later, in telling of the object of spirit communication, Silver Birch explained:

"We do not seek to terrify you with threats of punishment. We do not seek to make you craven cowards, living your lives because of fear.

"We strive to make you realise the latent divinity that is yours, that you may express more of the Great Spirit, that you may rise to greater heights and fill your minds with greater truth and wisdom.

"We urge you to be dissatisfied with what you have already received," he added, "because only through discontent and the desire to reach out can greater knowledge come. He who is satisfied stagnates: he who is discontented struggles towards greater freedom.

"We never say to you, 'Do not use your reason: have faith only.'

"We say, 'Use that which the Great Spirit has given you. Test us. Examine us. If aught that we say is debasing, cruel or immoral, then reject us.

"'If we seek always to teach you to live nobler lives, lives of greater self-sacrifice and of idealism, then surely that demonstrates that the hall-mark of the Great Spirit is stamped upon our teaching' . . .

"All we who are immersed in this great work often take for granted the things which were in former days a great revelation. To those who have dwelt in darkness for many years, and whose souls are ready, a few words of truth come as a blinding flash.

"If we raise up one soul, if we give comfort to one who mourns, if we give hope to one who is faint-hearted, if we give strength to one who is weary, then has it not been worth doing?

"While it is good to receive commendation, think of the many whom it disturbs, whom it puzzles, who are perplexed, who, bound to a creed, cannot escape—yet they hear the voice of freedom calling to their imprisoned souls and their minds struggle to be free.

"They are the ones for whom the message is intended, not those who can appreciate it, but those to whom it comes as an incentive to reach out to what before was unattainable. All truth is but a stepping stone."

"That is true," remarked a sitter.

"I know it is true," replied the guide. "If I did not know it, I would not say it.

"I say this in all humility—if you hear through the lips of the medium through whom I am privileged to address you that which makes your reason revolt, that which contradicts the love of the Great Spirit, that which is foolish, that which is an insult to your intelligence, then know that my day is done and I have failed.

"Though I have spoken to you many, many times, I do not think I have ever said anything which is contrary to the highest aspirations of the soul. For our appeal is always to the highest that is within you."

'You are the pioneers'

"Our work is to give that which has a purpose, a significance, so that, while it demonstrates the existence of law, it also enables comfort to be given and knowledge to be spread.

"Our work is not only to reveal the existence of laws beyond the physical, but to reveal truths of the Spirit.

"We have a gigantic system of misrepresentation to oppose. We have to undo the work of centuries. We have to destroy the superstructure of falsity that has been built upon the foundations of creeds.

"We are striving always to teach the chiidren of matter how to be free and how to bask in the sunlight of spiritual truth, how to cast off the serfdom of creedal slavery. That is not an easy task, for once the trappings of religion have mastered you, it takes a long time for spiritual truth to penetrate that thick wall of superstition.

"We strive always to reveal the religious significance of spiritual truth, for, when your world understands its spiritual import, there will be a revolution mightier than all the revolutions of war and blood.

"It will be a revolution of the soul and, all over the world, they will claim what is their due—the right to enjoy to the full the liberties of the Spirit. Away will go every restriction which has put fetters on them.

"You are the pioneers, helping to cut the road, smoothing away all the obstacles, so that those who come after you will have an easier path to travel. Those who should aid you in that task through spiritual blindness, range themselves as your enemies. That is their loss.

"Our allegiance is not to a creed, not to a book, not to a Church, but to the Great Spirit of life and to His eternal natural laws."

Chapter Six

'THE LAW IS PERFECT'

SILVER Birch's circle sat for decades and received many visitors. So it was that the issues put to the guide were as varied as the guests who made their way to the medium's NW London apartment.

Once, for example, the spirit teacher was asked if he would comment on vegetarianism.

"I know I will be unpopular with some," he said. "But if I have to tread on corns, then I must. There can be no argument that, for the ideal medium, abstinence from alcoholic liquor, from flesh foods, from tobacco and from anything which degrades the human body is better for the developing spirit. The spirit can only express itself in your world through a physical body. The higher the quality of the physical body, the greater can be the expression of the spirit. Therefore anything which coarsens that body, anything which gives it wrongful stimulation, is a hindrance and not a help to the spiritual body, of which the physical counterpart is its temple.

"Now you can answer the question for yourself. Can the flesh of animals, can the stimulation of tobacco and alcohol help the unfoldment of psychic and spiritual faculties that you possess? Of course they cannot. Naturally, if these things are done in moderation, they will do little harm. But for the ideal medium, it is better that he should confine himself to the fruits of the earth."

This led to another point. "Is it wrong," asked the questioner, "to kill animals for food and clothes when apparently it is nature's way for animals to kill and eat each other?"

"All these things are comparative and are all part of evolution," said the guide. "We are told that Nature is red in tooth and claw. That is part of the evolution of Nature—and no spirit teacher has claimed that Nature has reached perfection, for Nature is still evolving. In the ideal—and I always answer what the ideal should be—it is wrong to kill for your food, for your clothing or for your shelter. But in an undeveloped world the full ideal cannot always be realised, but that is no reason why there should not be a striving towards the ideal, which is perfection.

"If there must be killing, let it be painless. Abolish the cruelty. If you cannot in one step reach the stage where mankind knows that to kill for food is wrong, then make the killing as painless as you can. You are in a changing world and we are preaching ideals, ideals that we know are not possible of immediate attainment. But we should be failing in our mission as teachers if we did not give you an ideal to strive for. Your standards must be raised, not lowered."

A highly unusual point was put to Silver Birch when a guest asked if hypnotism "is a good subject for study."

"If the man who hypnotises is of good intent, and desires to use his power for service—then, of course, it is good," came the spirit answer. "The hypnotist is only tapping some of the latent powers of the soul."

"What is it that the hypnotist gets in touch with?" asked the visitor.

"The over-self, which is the same as the Great Spirit within," said Silver Birch. "I have often told you that, if you could realise the power within you, and if you would use that power, it would enable you to overcome every difficulty.

"Those powers can be contacted by development, by attuning yourselves to higher vibrations, by living better lives of service, by raising your spirits. The more you are of the earth, the lower are the vibrations to which you respond. The higher you reach out in self-abnegation, the higher are the vibrations to which you respond and the more the Great Spirit that is within you can express itself."

"Is the Great Spirit within a separate entity, capable of reasoning, thinking and acting independently of the conscious self?" the guide was asked.

"No, it is conditioned by that part of the conscious mind which is now expressed through your material body," was the reply. "It is only conditioned in that way while you are living in the world of matter. It is not conditioned under the influence of hypnotism, because the hypnotist is like the gaoler who opens the prison door and allows the prisoner to escape.

"If the hypnotist is of good intent, he can perform great service, for he can stimulate the divine within. But, also, he can stimulate the animal within. But always remember that the consciousness which you now express is but a very small fragment of the consciousness which one day you will express."

"That makes us a little dissatisfied," commented a sitter.

"Yes, it is good to be dissatisfied," returned Silver Birch. "Smug satisfaction is no incentive to progress."

Remarking that he was always pleased to answer any question, Silver Birch said, "Knowledge is given to us, not to keep to ourselves but to give to others, for in giving we make ourselves more accessible to the fountain of knowledge again.

"Knowledge, when you give it away, does not make you poorer, but increases. When you give away spiritual things, you are richer."

One present wanted to know the effect on the mind of Christianity and other orthodox beliefs. The guide replied:

"The bondage of creeds is one of your world's afflictions. It is worse than pestilence and disease, far worse than the physical sufferings of the body through illness, for it is an affliction of the soul. It puts the spirit in blinkers.

"And yet your world clings to creed when it has at its disposal the infinite wisdom of the Great Spirit," remarked the guide. "There are some who are only happy whilst they are in prison. Liberty is only for those who know how to enjoy liberty.

"Rejoice that you have escaped from the thraldom of creed. Rejoice, and strive to elevate others that they too may escape."

Questioned as to the value of suffering, Silver Birch said:

"Every experience is part of the pattern of your life. You try to judge eternity by the temporal happenings. You see in matter apparent confusion, but you do not realise that a divine thread runs throughout all your lives.

"In the great universe where harmony is the law, each one of you contributes to the plan. The events in your lives, sometimes of bitterness and despair, of pain and misery, all play their part in preparing the soul gradually for the path that is being trodden.

"The darkness and the light, the shadow and the sunshine, are all but reflections of one whole. Without shadow there could be no light and without light there could be no shadow. The difficulties of life are steps which enable the soul to rise.

"Difficulties, obstacles, handicaps—these are the trials of the soul. And when it conquers them all, it rises stronger, more purified, deepened in intensity and more highly evolved.

"Do you think that the latent powers of the soul, infinite in their possibilities of expression, could realise themselves without difficulty and pain, without shadow, without sorrow, and without suffering and misery? Of course not.

"The joy and the laughter can only be enjoyed to the full

when once you have drained the cup of sorrow to the dregs, for as low as you can fall in the scale of life so correspondingly you can rise. The more you have tasted and experienced that which seems the shadow of earthly life, the more you will appreciate, because of it, the greater joys of the sunshine.

"Your experiences are all part of your evolution. One day, freed from the trammels of flesh, with eyes not clouded by matter, you will look back in retrospect and view the life you have lived on earth. And out of the jigsaw of all the events, you will see how every piece fits into its allotted place, how every experience was a lesson to quicken the soul and to enable it to have greater understanding of its possibilities.

"The greatest trials that we on this side of life have to endure are when we see the ones we love in your world, who are linked with us with bonds of affection, having to endure suffering and we realise that we must not stretch out a hand to aid them, that it is necessary for their soul evolution."

Silver Birch declared that everyone had his trials. The important thing was the way they were faced.

"There is no experience that comes to the human soul," he said, "which, rightly understood and rightly faced, does not leave you better for it. Can you contemplate a world of matter where there were no difficulties, no trials, no troubles, no pain, no suffering? There would be no evolution. There would be nothing to surmount. You would decay."

"If suffering is essential to the soul's progress, why are spiritual healers allowed to alleviate it?" asked a sitter.

"Because the healing enables the soul to find itself," said the guide. "Great as is the work of healing, there is a greater work that healers perform—they touch the souls of those who come near them and enable them to find themselves."

"In comparison with this, would you regard the healing of bodies as less important?" the guide was asked.

"Yes," was the reply. "You who dwell in bodies of matter

think only of lives in your world. We who have left the earth place it in its proper proportion as only a speck of your infinite lives. All your focus is wrong.

"You see a poor soul suffering and, very rightly, the compassion rises in your breast. I do not condemn that. But you only think in terms of the suffering, not realising that the time spent in that suffering is infinitesimal compared with the compensating joys.

"To you, the shadows always seem longer than the sunlight —but they are not.

"But you must also realise that not all who are sick can be healed by healers. There are laws at work, and some people the healer cannot cure.

"It is no accident that when the time is ripe the sick man is healed, just as it is no accident that when the soul is ready for its new experience beyond the gate of 'death' the physical body drops away. It is all determined by law. But you play your part in that law, for you are all parts of the Great Spirit."

"If healing only comes when the soul has earned it, by paying off its debts, would not the body be healed without going to a healer?" was the next question.

"If all the debts were paid—and they are never paid—you would have reached the stage where pain could not touch you," said Silver Birch, "for your body would be perfect. But you always contract debts, in your world and in mine."

"But what part does the healer play, if it is all worked out according to law?" persisted the sitter.

"When people are ready to be healed, the healer is brought to them, or they are brought to the healer," the guide replied. "Have you been so long with us and do not know how people are brought together? The evolution they have reached determines the healer who will be able to heal them.

"The Great Spirit cannot forget. The law is perfect, automatic in its operation. Nobody can evade the law. Even free will is a law, and its operation is known to those who can see, because they have reached that stage of evolution, the operation of that law."

A sitter objected that the operation of free will seemed contrary to law, as if choice were determined it could not be free.

"You can only exercise your free will according to the stage of evolution you have reached," replied the guide. "It would be impossible for you to do anything but that which you do, because it is determined by the stage of evolution of your soul."

"Would that apply in the case of a person whose mind was unbalanced?" Silver Birch was asked.

"When your mind becomes unbalanced, it is only because of something you have done. That is still law. Your mind being unbalanced is only the effect."

"But if our choice is determined by law, how do our experiences affect our evolution?" queried a sitter. "Would not that make our evolution automatic also?"

"No, you forget that you are part of the Great Spirit and have an infinity of divinity to express," answered the spirit teacher. "As that divinity is expressed, so you become accessible to higher laws—which do not contravene other laws, but are only accessible to you as your evolution unfolds.

"There is no limit in infinity. There is no limit to the perfection of beauty, to the splendour of music, and the higher the soul is raised in the scale of evolution, the greater is the world of beauty and harmony available to it. As you rise, so a greater field of harmony awaits the evolved soul.

"You are not conscious of the higher whilst you are in the lower, but you are conscious of the lower whilst you are in the higher. Whilst all the laws that control every aspect of that harmony are automatic in their operation, they are not available to you until you have reached them by soul growth."

"But is not our future growth determined by our past soul growth?"—"No. Your past growth places you in the position of choosing future growth. But you can delay it."

"Then the operation of free will is not automatic?"—"Yes. What you will do at any moment is determined by the interplay of laws, each of which is automatic in its operation. And your choice is determined by the way that your consciousness responds at that stage of evolution. The soul, if it is aware of itself, chooses that which will advance its evolution."

"Can the soul choose to delay its growth?"—"You can only delay the physical consciousness expressed through your physical brain."

Recalling Silver Birch's comment that some sufferers could not hope to get relief from a healer because they were not ready for healing, one of the sitters remarked that this seemed to him to be "tragic."

"What will happen to them, do you think?" asked the guide.

"They will pass on, I suppose," said the sitter.

"And is that a tragedy?" asked Silver Birch. "I am 'dead.' I do not find it tragic. You think of physical things only.

"What a funny world you live in! You are all afraid of the greatest experience in life, all afraid of being released from prison, all afraid of being free. Is the bird afraid to leave its cage? Why are you afraid to leave your cages?"

"But a mother, for instance, would not want to leave her baby," said the questioner.

"You think only of your three-score-years-and-ten. Can you judge infinity by worldly things?

"Do not judge the Great Spirit by the infinitesimal physical world in which you live. You have no measure of comparison. How can you, who have only seen one of the lowest planes of life, understand the greatest spheres of expression."

This raised another question. "If those who are not ready to be healed pass on, then they enjoy the life of the spirit world," said a sitter. "Those who have reached the stage when they are ready to be healed have to stay in this world. It seems that the less evolved are better off than the more evolved."

"When you are ready to be healed, it means that the time for you to come to the spirit world is not yet, that the experience necessary for the soul through suffering of the body is over. But there are other experiences in the world of matter which the soul must have before it is ready to enter its new life. The physical suffering of the body is not the limit of human experience!"

One sitter was still not satisfied with Silver Birch's comments on orthodox Christianity. "There are plenty of good Christians," he objected.

"They would have been good just the same, whether they were Christians or not," said the guide.

"But are not some good because they try to follow the teachings of Jesus?" asked the sitter.

"When your world emulates the Nazarene, a new chapter will have begun in history," replied Silver Birch. "It has not happened yet. I do not see any signs of it. Do not speak to me of 'Christians,' whose lives mock the one they profess to serve.

"Did not the Nazarene say, 'Not every one that saith unto me, Lord, Lord, shall enter into the kingdom of heaven; but he that doeth the will of my Father which is in heaven'?"

"Yet there are thousands of Christians who believe the creeds superficially and who yet live very good lives and who are unselfish," said the sitter, mentioning the name of a famous parson as an example.

"He is not a good Christian," said Silver Birch. "He is a bad Christian, but a good man.

"Remember this, every creed is a fetter on the soul. Men are not good because of creed, but in spite of creed. In the name of creed they have killed one another and they have burned one another. Anything which binds, which cramps the soul, which prevents it from having full expression, must be swept away."

The sitter, still not satisfied, spoke of priests who go to leper colonies to help the sufferers there.

"They do not go because of creed," said the guide, "but because the soul wishes to serve. Religion is beyond creed. Creed is not religion."

During another discusion the subject of faith was raised. The guide gave his view, saying:

"Faith that is faith alone sometimes fails when the winds of bitter experience blow. But the faith that is born of knowledge provides a foundation which is so strong that no wind of circumstance can disturb it.

"Blessed are those who believe and have not yet seen, but thrice blessed are they who know and, because they know, place their faith in that which is not yet revealed to them, because they know that the laws of the universe are operated by a power which is love and wisdom.

"How simple are the things that we try to teach you, and yet they would say that we are evil ones! All we seek to reveal is the operation of natural law, so that you may regulate your lives with it and earn the peace which comes from within by placing yourselves in harmony with the Great Spirit of Life."

'Thou art limitless and infinite'

"Oh, Great White Spirit, Thou Who art the Lord and Arbiter of all life, and in Whose kingdom there is no death, we seek to reveal Thee Who art the infinite Spirit that broodeth over all things, that dost reveal Thyself in the mighty panorama of the operation of natural law.

"We reveal Thee as the Great Spirit of perfect justice and wisdom, Who is immanent in all life and Who is expressed in every living breathing thing.

"Oh, Great White Spirit, Thou art limitless and infinite, beyond the understanding of Thy children, but yet Thou art known, because Thou art seen in every expression of life, whether it be life in the planes of matter or life in the realms of spirit.

"Thou art heard in the song of birds, Thou art seen in the twinkling of the stars, in the glistening of the raindrops, in the flash of the lightning. Thou art in the murmur of the brook, in the drone of the bees, in the nodding of the trees. Thou art in the roll of the thunder and in the roar of the mighty sea. Thou art in the rising sun and in the pale reflection of the moon.

"Thou art in every phase of life, but Thou art closest in the human spirit as it stirs itself to reveal Thy love and Thy goodness in acts of service, self-sacrifice and idealism.

"And we, who are Thy messengers from the realms of the higher life, seek to reveal the operation of laws which have been known to a few in the days gone by, but which are now being revealed to those who can discern Thy plan beyond the confines of matter. We seek to reveal the existence of Thy spirit as it is expressed within all Thy children.

"Released from the bonds of matter and now operating in the greater world, we return according to Thy law to demonstrate that love continues and seeketh its own, to bring comfort and assurance, guidance and hope, knowledge and inspiration, wisdom and truth.

"In the rending of the veil and in the uniting of love, Thy children of earth may learn to recognise that great power of the Spirit which is latent within them, that they may be inspired and that they may be led to dedicate their lives to Thy service and to the service of the ones who suffer, so that they may express Thy divinity in their daily lives and exhibit Thy spirit to all.

"In that spirit, we come back so that we may render service whenever we can, seeking only to strengthen the bonds that bind all peoples together and make them realise the unity that is behind all life. May that power express itself in all those channels who seek to become Thy temples on earth. This is the prayer of Thy Indian servant who seeks to serve."

Chapter Seven

'THE EPITOME OF PERFECT LOVE'

THOUGH in recent years Silver Birch made a cassette recording—it has been heard by countless folk in countless lands—turning the clock back ever further the guide once recorded his voice onto a gramophone record.

Sadly the first record he made was a failure, from a reproduction point of view, because the microphone was placed too far away. The guide made no complaint. Instead, he started straight away on another record.

"What shall I talk about?" he said when was asked to make a second disc. His first talk had been one of comfort to mourners.

"Why not talk about the new world?" suggested Hannen Swaffer.

Without hesitation, Silver Birch started a talk on the new world—which was of exactly the right length for the record, which is no longer available. That was the remarkable aspect about every spirit address—there were four altogether, two prayers and two talks. They were all of exactly the right length!

So that the guide would know when to start recording and when to finish, it was arranged that a sitter should count up to nine then the apparatus was switched on and the guide started to talk. Half a minute before the recording was due to finish, the medium was touched—and the guide had so arranged everything that he finished in each case almost on the last second. And yet, he said, it was not rehearsed.

"I pray to the Great White Spirit of life," Silver Birch

began, making the first record, "Thou Who art the King of kings, the divine Architect, the infinite Intelligence behind perfect law. Thou art omniscient, omnipotent. Thou art ever present, for Thy spirit fills the whole universe and all is a reflection of Thee. But Thy spirit is shown in the lives of those who strive to render service, for there Thy divinity finds its fullest expression, as reaching out they fight all vested interest, all hatred, all cruelty, all superstition and all the ignorance that belongs to the darkness.

"We pay tribute to Thee Who art the epitome of perfect love and wisdom because we seek to reveal Thee as Thou art in all Thy majesty, for Thou hast been misinterpreted through the ages, except by a few who possessed the open vision and the clear-seeing eye. Thou art not a despotic, vindictive, jealous tyrant. Thou art the Great Spirit of all life, for Thy spirit is within every child in the universe and they are linked with Thee throughout all eternity. Because of Thy spirit they live; because of Thy spirit they exist in the world beyond death."

During the last half-minute, it appeared to sitters that the guide would not finish in time. That half-minute seemed almost as long as the previous two and a half minutes since the recording began. But Silver Birch knew how much he could say in the time! Another disc was put on the machine, the sitter counted up to nine and "I whom you call Silver Birch desire to send a message to those whose eyes are filled with tears and whose hearts are heavy with sadness because they mourn the ones they love, whom they think death has robbed them of their presence. I who have lived in the world of spirit for many years wish to tell them that death cannot divide those whom love has joined. Love breaks all barriers; love always findeth its own.

"Do not weep because the one you love is taken from a world of cruelty, of misunderstanding, of ignorance, into a larger life where all its innate qualities can find richer expression. Do not be bitter because the Great Spirit has transplanted a flower from your garden into His, where it can shed a greater fragrance, freed from all the limitations and restrictions of your world. Try to understand that death is part of the law of life, for life and death are both servants of the Great Spirit, and both are used to teach His laws to those who do not yet properly understand them. Dry your tears. Your sorrow should not be, for the one you love is always close to you. Death cannot destroy love; love is infinite as the Great Spirit is infinite too."

"Shall we play it over to you?" asked one of the recorders. "We can play it once without hurting it for reproduction."

"If it can only be played once, I would rather you did not play it now but waited until my medium comes out of trance, so that he can hear it too," said the guide, not wishing to prevent his medium from hearing the voice.

"Well, we can play it twice without damaging it," said the recorder. Then it was realised the voice was too faint. The guide's voice is much lower than the medium's and did not register so well. In a test made earlier in the evening, the microphone was placed in the best position to record the medium's voice.

"Can you repeat what was said?" someone asked. "No, that is not possible," said Silver Birch. "But I will start again." So the other record was started—and the guide prayed:

"I pray to the Great White Spirit. Oh, Great White Spirit, Thou Who art the divine Architect, Thou Who art the King of all kings, the infinite Intelligence behind all life, we seek to reveal Thee as Thou art—perfect law. Thou hast been misunderstood and misinterpreted throughout the ages. Men have thought of Thee as a cruel, bloodthirsty, vindictive, jealous tyrant, with partiality to those who made sacrifices to Thee.

"Men have approached Thee in fear and trembling, afraid of Thy wrath. We seek to reveal Thee as Thou art—the epitome of perfect love and wisdom, for Thou dost desire to reveal Thyself through the operation of all Thy laws, so that Thy children may find in life its fullness, its richness and its plenteous bounty. We desire to bring into operation the laws that belong to Thy spiritual domain, so that they may inspire all people of good will to greater efforts and greater service, that they may free your world from all its inequalities, all its injustices and all that stands in the way of Thy kingdom of heaven being made manifest on earth. To that end we pray and labour."

The second half of the second record was spoiled when Silver Birch made a mistake in a word—he said "service" instead of "surface." "That spoils it," he remarked and waited for a new disc to be put on the machine before he started again.

"When all your world is full of darkness," he began without hesitation, "and fear reigns in the heart of man, and the children of your world know not where to turn for guidance and comfort, we who live in the larger life and who can see beyond the confines of matter stress the note of confidence and tell you all is well.

"You are witnessing the birth of a new order and all around you are the signs that the old world, founded on selfishness, materialism, greed, avarice and cruelty, is dying. You who call yourselves Spiritualists are the custodians of a great truth, for you are the sentries guarding the outposts, helping to forge the new era. Think of yourselves as soldiers of the Great Spirit, fighting the greatest fight of all, for you are helping to vanquish all the forces that belong to the darkness of man's ignorance and brought war, misery, chaos and bankruptcy to your world.

"You are helping to shape a new world in which all the

children of the Great Spirit will share to the full the richness
of the bounty He has freely given."

'The Great Spirit of all life'

"Oh, Great White Spirit, how shall we describe Thy infinity,
Thy wisdom, the fullness of Thy love, the supremacy of Thy
inspiration? How shall we describe Thee, Who art limitless,
to those who are encased in bodies of matter?

"How can we reveal Thee in Thy fullness when Thou hast
been distorted and 'revealed' as a jealous, cruel and vindictive
God? Yet Thou art the Great Spirit of all life, Who pulsates
through every manifestation of Nature, Who dost reveal
Thyself in every breath of the universe.

"We rejoice in the knowledge that has been vouchsafed of
Thee, in the wisdom that has been given to those who could
raise themselves above the vibrations of matter, and see
spiritual truths with eyes that pierce the physical veil. We
rejoice because ears, attuned to the higher vibrations of Spirit,
have caught the revelation that comes from Thee and have
revealed Thee as a God of love, wisdom and justice.

"Oh, Great White Spirit, we rejoice that, all through the
ages, there have been those who have welcomed the
messengers of Spirit, that there have been those inspired from
the finer realm who have been in the world to spread Thy
truth in the dark places of the world of matter, to bring Thy
light and Thy knowledge where ignorance and superstition
have reigned.

"We rejoice in the few who have stood as testimony to the
power of the Spirit and have sought to uplift, to reform, to
inspire and to make the world of matter a place fitting for the
children of Thee to dwell in.

"We rejoice, too, that Thou hast entrusted to us the task of bringing Thy truth once again to a world full of misery, pain and sorrow, that, throughout all the chaos and confusion, those who are ready to lead Thy children out of the morass that they have created are enabled to be filled with Thy power of the Spirit, to realise that they are encompassed by Thy messengers and that in all their efforts Thy power flows through them.

"And we, who strive to bring to the world of matter that knowledge of spiritual things which is the natural heritage of all religions, pray that all that stands between the fullness of Thy power flowing between the two spheres of existence may be abolished, that all the veils of superstition, of ignorance, of prejudice, of intolerance, of bigotry, may be stripped away and Thy children stand in the light of Thy divine truth.

"May Thy children realise the purpose for which Thou hast placed them in the world of matter, the tasks which Thou hast entrusted them to perform, so that, in realising these things, they may live their lives in the service of one another, driving out all wars and rumours of wars, all fears, all bitterness, all darkness, so that Thy kingdom may reign in peace and in plenty.

"This is the prayer of Thy Indian servant, who seeks to serve Thee by serving Thy children."

Chapter Eight

'DO NOT DESPAIR'

BRITAIN—and indeed the whole Commonwealth—was plunged into a crisis in far-off 1936 when King Edward VIII announced his abdication so he could marry American divorcee Wallis Simpson. Never before had modern-day monarchy faced such a testing, turbulent time.

Not surprisingly this headline-making event was raised at the Hannen Swaffer home circle where Silver Birch gave a spirit view of the abdication.

"The conditions of your world have been very difficult," he said, "but now they begin to clear away. I want to remind you all that there is a great lesson to be learned from it.

"In all moments of crisis, fix your minds upon the eternal things of the Spirit. Do not dwell too much on the kingdom of empires and dominions, but on the Kingdom of Heaven, which has yet to descend on earth.

"Do not have excessive adoration for those who are only men. Remember that there is only one King in the universe, the King of all life, Whose kingdom embraces every child of the Great Spirit and Who wants all His plenteous bounty distributed freely.

"Do not let your attention be diverted, because of glamour, from the great eternal realities. Remember the conditions of those who dwell in misery and in darkness, those who lack food, those whom the sun seldom reaches, those who are prevented from breathing as they should the air which comes from the Great Spirit of life.

"Remember the greater tasks, the greater problems.

Remember the masses who cry out, whose pain, bitterness and sorrow are far, far greater than the difficulties of only one. That is the great lesson for all in your world of matter to learn."

At this point Hannen Swaffer asked whether his view of the crisis—it was printed in "Psychic News"—was too harsh. The paper swiftly received several letters, one saying that Swaffer's stand was "The most heartless thing that has ever been written." Another declared that his comments were "ungentlemanly, unmanly, ungenerous and un-Christian."

"No," replied Silver Birch. "When you speak truth, truth finds its way into their hearts. Sometimes it meets with the resistance of superstition and prejudice. But those walls will crumble gradually. You could not have said it many years ago, but you say it today.

"A few complain, but they are nothing. They are those within whose minds traditional things die hard. They do not reason with logic and understanding. You told them of the natural laws. They are the only ones that matter.

"When the passions created in men's breasts die down, they will have to confront reality. That is your task in your world of matter—to tear away the veils of illusion and to reveal truth. Some cannot behold truth's blinding light, but it is of no account. They are not ready.

"The truth reigns supreme. Ignorance flees before its approach. It is because our message is true that we one day will reign supreme—not we who are the instruments, but that which we represent, the love of the Great Spirit, the infinity of His bounty, the love, the wisdom, the knowledge that watches over all mankind.

"Away must go every obstacle that prevents the fullness of the Great Spirit being revealed. Away must go all servitude. Away must go all barriers. That is the task upon which we are all engaged.

"I only try to tell you a few of the things that I have learned, because I know that they can help you even if they make you examine again the fundamental principles of life.

"Sometimes, when you are engrossed in your daily tasks and the problems of your world surround you, you are apt to forget the great eternal spiritual principles upon which all life is based. If I remind you of these things, they help you to focus your minds so that you can get the true balance and are able to render still greater service.

"Your world has yet to learn so much. The greater the responsibility, the greater the sacrifice. The greater the knowledge that you possess, the greater the responsibility. You can gain nothing without a price. There is a price always to be paid."

A month earlier Silver Birch gave his then customary Armistice Day message. He told those present:

"I want you all to remember when, in a few days' time, the thoughts of the whole of your nation are centred on the many who laid down their bodies of matter in service, that it is a great reminder to you all of the way in which millions of the children of the Great Spirit have been for years betrayed by those who lead in the affairs of men.

"The sacrifices have all been in vain, and the sacred reminder comes to each one of you to realise that there are only a few very simple ways by which peace, harmony and happiness can reign.

"You build up systems based on greed and selfishness and, as a result, you reap war and poverty, starvation and misery, distress and chaos. And then you ask us how we can help you, when all the time the message of the Spirit has been forgotten and neglected, even by those who should preach the word of the Great Spirit.

"Temporal power is as naught beside spiritual realities, and, although many sneer at the things of the Spirit, the solution of all the troubles of your world will only be found when all people, in the spirit of goodwill, apply spiritual truth to material problems.

"You are nearer disaster today than you were when it was announced that war had ceased. You are nearer to grave and terrible troubles. The world is heading straight for that which spells bloodshed, great bloodshed.

"I speak with gravity because of that which I know. It may be that the world will be saved from itself, but only if the efforts of all those who seek to serve, not to aggrandise self, triumph over the power of greed and selfishness. Peace will not come to your world from war. Happiness will not come from misery. Laughter cannot come from tears of sorrow.

"There is plenty for all. But greed stands in the way. Those who seek to rule by the sword must perish by the sword. That same truth prevails today.

"But, throughout all the darkness, there is a glimmer of hope. Do not despair. Hold fast to that which you know to be true."

A year later in another Armistice Day message the guide referred to the Spanish Civil War in which, incidentally, Maurice Barbanell and his wife were inadvertently caught up! Happily both escaped injury and were escorted to the French border by gun-toting soldiers. The ever-eloquent guide commented:

"Each succeeding year makes the futility of this human sacrifice more apparent. Your world will pay for just two minutes of its time and silent tribute in memory of the 'glorious dead,' and after that they will be forgotten for another year, until they are taken off the shelf and dusted once again.

"Their sacrifices were all in vain. They have been crucified for nineteen years. The Great War! Its greatness consisted in the amount of slaughter, wasted slaughter. The Great War, that was to end all war! How hollow, how full of mockery do those words sound!

"Do you not consider that those who made every sacrifice that they could make in the world of matter, even to laying down their physical lives, have not spent years in bitter disillusionment? They were cut off in the prime of earthly life. They were sent unprepared into the world of spirit. They passed on cheerfully for an ideal, that your civilisation might be saved, and they have been betrayed ever since.

"War has not been driven from the face of the earth, for, even as you will pay tribute to the 'fallen dead,' as you call them, of your last war, there will be no armistice in the East or in Spain, where the killing will continue even without a cessation of two minutes.

"Does your world of matter realise that peace can only come from the application of spiritual laws to worldly matters?

"It is selfishness that brings not only war, with its train of bloodshed, misery and weeping, but chaos, confusion, disaster and bankruptcy.

"They must learn that only by substituting service for selfishness can peace come, that the old ideas of materialism and power and desires to aggrandise nations must be swept away and in their place there must reign the desire to live for one another, the stronger to help the weaker, the richer to give to the poorer.

"Do not insult those who have been translated to spirit realms with tributes that come from the lips and not from the heart.

"All other methods have been tried and they have failed you. But not yet has the application of spiritual truths been tried. Unless your world does so, it will continue with war and bloodshed that will, in the end, destroy your much vaunted civilisation."

Perhaps at this point it is pertinent to include the guide's words upon civilisation. Asked to comment on it, Silver Birch replied that free will "is a gift of the Great Spirit, but if it is not used aright then the price must be paid.

"The laws must be obeyed," he went on. "If the world lives with the law, it reaps the benefits. If it lives against the law, it reaps the results. One way brings peace and happiness and plenty, the other way misery and war and bloodshed and chaos.

"We are despised in your world of matter by those who should be the leaders of the children of the Great Spirit. We are rejected by those who should welcome us because we come in the name of the Great Spirit and His love. Filled with the desire to serve, we seek to reveal those laws and that power which will show your world how to save itself.

"And those who are steeped in the ignorance of spiritual blindness, and who surround themselves with ceremony and ritual, and at the same time deny the power of the Great Spirit to descend today, must pay the price.

"We are the friends of all who seek to serve. We are the enemies only of those who seek to destroy. We come on wings of love and service ready to help wherever we can. That is the great task that we all have to perform.

"Your world pays too much attention to old fables because they are old. Truth and age do not always march together. I know it is difficult to surrender the dearly held beliefs learned in the days of childhood, but when the soul becomes free it must discard all that reason rejects. How many are prepared to do that?"

"It does not occur to many people to test their beliefs by reason," said a sitter.

"No, they prefer the shelter of that which they have known for so long rather than journey into the speculative unknown," the guide remarked. "And remember, also, your world does not acclaim its pioneers with much applause. It usually condemns them."

Another sitter wanted to know why so much was said about a spirit plan to help the world, "and yet we see such little apparent result of it?"

"You do not see the results of a Plan," said the guide, "because you look at these things with the eyes of matter. You judge progress in relation to your own short span of life, but we see progress because we look at things from another plane.

"We see the spread of knowledge, a greater understanding of spiritual things, a rise of tolerance, an increase of good will, a breaking down of barriers of ignorance and superstition and fear and spiritual slavery.

"It is not as if there were to be a sudden revolution. That could never happen, because all spiritual growth must be slow and progressive.

"Do not think that there is need for despair. There is on one hand—when you see the growing masses of materialistic forces—but on the other hand there is growing hope as the light of spiritual truth penetrates the fog of materialistic selfishness. And, as long as knowledge spreads, truth will be victorious.

"That is why our message is so important. It is not for us—it is for you. It is we who strive to serve you, to make your world realise the price it must pay for its selfishness, for its wanton ignorance, its deliberate cruelty. We strive to serve you, to help you, because we love you.

"We are not evil spirits, seeking to lure you on to paths of destruction. We do not seek to make you debase yourselves, to practise cruelty or sin. Rather do we strive to make you realise the divinity that is yours, the powers of the Great Spirit that you possess, how you can practise the law of service and help the Plan of the Great Spirit."

At a different gathering the guide was asked if it would be a good thing "if our present civilisation were destroyed."

"It is much better for your civilisation to be saved, even in spite of itself," was the spirit sage's reply.

"Don't you think it has gone so far wrong that it would be better to start all over again?" the sitter persisted.

"No, because the light of spiritual truth is breaking in upon your world," said Silver Birch. "Where there are channels for the power of the spirit to penetrate, so there comes to you that energy that enables your world to exist.

"Your world must realise that it depends for its existence upon the reservoir of spirit."

Another sitter suggested that Silver Birch was rather harsh in his declaration that the sacrifices of those "killed" in the war were all in vain. He thought it would hurt many people to be told that.

"Sometimes stark truth is bitter and hurts," said the guide, "but, because it is true, it will do good."

"But did not any good at all come out of their sacrifices?" the sitter asked.

"I can see none," answered Silver Birch. "Your world of matter is nearer chaos today, and is more filled with destruction, than it was when your 'Great War' began."

"Can so much heroism be spent in vain?" the sitter queried. "Is there no spiritual repercussion?"

"There is on the part of the individuals who made the sacrifice, because their motive was good," the spirit guide replied. "But do not forget that your world has betrayed them. It has made their sacrifice pointless, because it has continued in its materialism."

"Is it of any use that these Armistice services should go on, year after year?" asked another sitter.

"It is better to remember those you call dead for two minutes than not to think of them at all," added the guide. "But I do not see what good can come when you celebrate the Armistice with a display of military might, with rifles and bayonets, with soldiers, with the firing of maroons and with all that comes with war. Could you not have an Armistice that was a spiritual service?"

"Are you in favour of the continuance of Spiritualist services of remembrance on that date?" was another point put to him.

"Wherever truth is expressed good is done, if speeches are given as an incentive to service. Vain speeches that lead to nothing are valueless. It is not sufficient to have speeches, and for audiences to be smugly satisfied with the feeling that they are in favour of peace.

"I want them active. I want them serving. I want them uplifting the weak. I want them healing the sick. I want them comforting the mourner. I want them sheltering the homeless. I want them to put an end to all the abuses that are a blot on your world of matter. Only through service can peace come. It will not come until all are imbued with the ideals of service, until all practise service."

At the same circle gathering the guide was asked if he agreed with the Pacifist movement which today is probably stronger than ever before.

"I belong to no party," he replied. "I wear no label. I see service, motive. Do not be confused with titles. Ask what is the aim, what is the desire, because there are men of honesty and good intent even in opposing camps. The teaching that we have to give you is very simple, but it requires courage to put it into practice.

"Whenever a start is made, whenever there is the determination that comes with knowledge of the spirit and the truths of the spirit, whenever service and not selfishness is applied to all the affairs of everyday life in the world of matter, then you will have peace and concord in your world.

"It will not come through any party, but through the children of the Great Spirit who, realising these things are true, apply them in their lives, in their politics, in their factories, in their governments, in their international transactions.

"We can enunciate principles that we know are founded on truth, and tell you with certainty that their application will bring results. You are in the realm of matter. Yours is the responsibility. We can only strive to guide you, with all our love and helpfulness, and co-operate with you whenever your feet are on the right paths . . .

"So many in your world cannot get out of the groove in which they live. Sometimes the groove is religious, sometimes it is political, sometimes it is a self-made prison that has no reality beyond the imagination of its creator.

"Learn to be free. Do not imprison yourself. Do not hedge yourself around and refuse to allow new inspiration to come to you. Truth is a constant search. Its boundaries are ever widening, for as the soul evolves the mind responds."

"How can one become free?" asked a sitter.

"You are never completely free, because the measure of your freedom is related to the growth of your soul," said the guide. "You become free when you realise there is no limitation to knowledge, truth, wisdom, growth. You become free when you discard at once that which you know in your heart is false, that which reason rejects, because your intelligence cries out in revolt. You become free when you are not afraid to discard error in the face of new light. But how many are prepared to do that?"

One present suggested that sometimes economic conditions prevented people from becoming free.

"No, for they cannot imprison the mind though they can imprison the body," said Silver Birch. "You imprison your own minds. There is knowledge for all when you are ready to seek knowledge, but *you* must journey on the great adventure.

"You must be prepared to start on a search where even

sometimes the boundaries are not known, sometimes be prepared for hazards and dangers, sometimes be prepared to walk in uncharted territory, yet always prepared to follow truth wherever she leads and to reject all that is false, no matter how old it may be."

'In the roar of the thunder'

"Oh, Great White Spirit, how shall we express the majesty of Thy love, the infinity of Thy wisdom, the splendour of Thy knowledge and inspiration? Thou art the great law of all life, the law that encompasses all life, whether it be life revealed in the majestic panorama of natural events, or whether it be life that is reflected in its most minute aspects.

"Thy law reigns supreme through every manifestation of life. Thou art expressed in all things, and nothing exists apart from Thee. Thou art in the beauty of the rising and the setting sun, in the pale reflection of the moon, in the glittering stars in the heavens, in the trilling songs of the birds, in the nodding of flowers, the rustling of pines, the splashing of the brook, the mighty ebb and flow of the ocean's tide.

"Thou art in the flash of the lightning, in the roar of the thunder. Thou art above as Thou art beneath. Thou art within as Thou art without. Thou art the Great Spirit, in Whose embrace is held all love, all power, all manifestation.

"And we, who are Thy instruments, charged to deliver Thy message, seek to reveal Thee in the fullness of Thy love, so that those who are still imprisoned in the flesh house of matter may recognise within themselves the realm of Thy spirit and know that they are spirit of Thy spirit, and that Thou has breathed into every one of them a portion of Thyself.

"Oh, Great White Spirit, in the world of matter that is filled with darkness and chaos, distrust and jealousy, suspicion and war, we pray that the floodgates of Thy revelation shall be opened, that the mighty power of Thy spirit shall descend on all those of good will and love, who seek to bring Thy message to all the nations, so that instead of living for self, they may learn to live for one another and bring Thy greater kingdom into operation on earth.

"And may all those channels which express Thy inspiration be free and pure, so that the fullness of Thy message may flow through them and that more and more of Thy children shall be brought within the orbit of the illumination of Thy truth.

"May they realise more and more what is the power that is round and about them. May they become conscious of that mighty power of the Spirit which has been sent in order to give them inspiration and guidance, to lead their feet on the pathway of service, so that they might express to the full the power of the Great Spirit which is within them."

Chapter Nine

'SPIRIT IS SUPERIOR'

WHILE the Roman Catholic Church admits of only three kinds of baptism—baptism by water, baptism by blood and baptism by desire—it leaves out the most essential form.

"You have all been baptised in the real meaning of the word—baptised in the spirit," declared Silver Birch at one circle gathering. "You have been born again. The soul has begun to lead you to find itself.

"The power of the Spirit is in your midst, and with it there comes not only reality, but certainty. It illumines the whole of your minds, fills your souls with peace and your hearts with love. It is the greatest manifestation of the Great Spirit."

One of the sitters, rather puzzled by some of the phrases in Silver Birch's invocations, asked, "Is the Great Spirit really in everything—in every stone, for instance?"

"The Great Spirit is in everything," the guide replied, "for nothing exists apart from the Great Spirit."

"Then is the Great Spirit responsible for earthquakes?" the sitter asked.

"The Great Spirit is the Law—the Law that controls all things," was the reply. "The Law governs all things. There is nothing in the universe which is outside the Law."

"I have often been puzzled by earthquakes," said the sitter, not quite satisfied with the guide's answer.

"I know that earthquakes and storms and lightning puzzle the brains of those in your world," said Silver Birch, "but they are all part of the universe. The universe is evolving, even as those who dwell in it are evolving. The world of matter is far from perfect yet—and it will not reach perfection. It will evolve higher and higher."

"Does that mean that the Great Spirit is evolving?" queried the sitter.

"No, the Great Spirit is the Law and the Law is perfect," replied Silver Birch. "But that part of the Great Spirit that is expressed in your world is subject to the evolution of that world as far as its expression is concerned.

"Remember that your world is evolving, and these things are the signs of its evolution. Your world was born in fire and tempest and is gradually evolving towards perfection.

"You cannot say that the Great Spirit is responsible for the beauty of the sunset and the sunrise, for the myriads of glittering stars in the firmament, for all the delightful songs of birds, and then say that the Great Spirit is not responsible for the storm and the lightning, the thunder and the rain. They are all part of the great law of the Great Spirit.

"In that sense, you might argue that the Great Spirit is responsible for those who are depraved, for those who are so unenlightened that they render harm to their brothers in your world.

"But to each one of you there is given that amount of free will which, as you evolve, you learn to exercise. The higher you evolve in the spiritual scale, the greater can you exercise your free will. You are your own limitation, but, because you are part of the Great Spirit, you can conquer all the difficulties and obstacles in your world.

"Spirit is superior to matter. Spirit is the king and matter is the servant. Spirit reigns supreme. It is the essence out of which all life is made, for spirit is life and life is spirit."

Silver Birch was asked whether free will was limited in the sense that there are definite tendencies of events in relation to individuals.

"There are tendencies, vibrations," replied Silver Birch,

"but these are not insuperable. You are surrounded by radiations and influences, much of which can affect your destiny, but the Great Spirit has provided you with part of Himself, a part of His spirit which, when your free will is properly used according to your evolution, can enable you to conquer all that stands in the way of the fullest expression of that part of the Great Spirit that is within you. For you are the Great Spirit and the Great Spirit is you."

When people say that communication with the "dead" retards them in their progress and drags them back unwillingly, they cannot know the facts.

"I love to hear the sound of your earthly voices," Silver Birch said. "It gives me much happiness. And I know that you like to hear from me, for we have much to learn from each other. I try very hard to learn from you of the things that belong to your world, so that I can add to my knowledge of earthly things and be of greater service if I can.

"Out of our talks there will come much work, for there is a great work for all of us to do—a work to which many of us who live in the realms of spirit have dedicated the whole of our lives.

"Part of that work will be accomplished here. You have seen some of it already. You have seen how we have been enabled to touch those who live not only in your own little country, but in other countries in your world"—Silver Birch was referring to the fact that there had frequently been visitors to the circle from overseas, some of whom had gone back and started home circles in their own countries as a result of their experiences here.

"That work will grow," he went on, "as the power of the Spirit grows here.

"Just go on with your faithful service and know that not one moment which is dedicated to our service is in vain, for our coming together always brings a rich blessing upon you who are in the world of matter and we who are released from the world's limitations. That blessing comes because our aim is not for ourselves but only for the service of others."

Like Baptism, the Church—and rightly—places great emphasis on the importance of marriage. But how does the spirit world view it? Silver Birch gave his opinion when addressing Vernon Moore, a circle member, and his fiancee, Frances, who for many years took down the guide's words in shorthand so they could be recorded, printed and sent out all over the world.

"I want you both to realise that you begin now the greatest adventure of all, for two lives that have pursued separate courses are now come together to begin a united life," the guide began. "Even as love has brought you to this place, even as love emanating from a world higher than yours guided your footsteps on paths of knowledge and truth, so has that same power brought you two together. Soon 'a man of God' will read a few words from a book and, according to your world of matter, you will be joined in the bonds of holy matrimony. But I say to you there are no bonds unless you bind one another with love and affection. There are no ties unless you wish to tie one another with love and affection.

"Do not think only in terms of two sharing one life from the physical aspect. Remember that you are two spiritual beings, both portions of the Great Spirit, now coming together with pledges to cherish, to love and to serve one another even as a great love from this world strives to serve you both. Remember that you are uniting two souls to adventure together and that we look not so much upon the material aspect but the spiritual, which to us is the enduring reality.

"Do not expect that you will escape occasional sadness and sorrow, difficulty, trial and test, for these are parts of your evolution. When they arise, as arise they inevitably must, face them with honesty and know that they help to quicken your character and to bring you closer together. There are many here who look forward with joy to a celebration which will duplicate the one you have in your church, but which will be sanctified in our world by ties we regard as more enduring, for the promises uttered audibly by word of mouth are as nothing compared with the unspoken pledges of the soul.

"You are richly blessed, for you have knowledge. I wish you, on behalf of many here who stand beside me, a safe journey through life's seas, happiness and joy abounding, but always ask you to remember that you continue to serve with the added fortification of love around you in the earthly world. Look up, not down, and realise that your strength cometh from above and from within your beings. Fortified by that knowledge, face the future knowing that all will be well and that where love dwells no harm can befall you. And I pray that the blessing of the Great Spirit rest with you and inspire you always in all aspects of your new life, and that you both shall for ever be conscious of the love that is round and about you."

The couple were members of Silver Birch's circle until 1981 when his medium passed on. Frequently the guide spoke of the natural law. Once Vernon, a former Methodist missionary, asked, "How are we to learn from natural law?"

"You learn through the evolution of your own spirit," replied the guide. "You learn first of all to discard all that which is false, all that which makes your reason revolt, all that which is not in consonance with the love and the wisdom of the Great Spirit.

"Before you learn, you must unlearn. You must discard all that which hinders your minds from thinking as they should. Thus your soul and your spirit grow and you are ready for higher knowledge.

"When you meet here, your soul is developing and you are becoming more accessible to the infinite wisdom of the Great

Spirit. You are learning about the operation of laws that control spiritual phenomena.

"You are being taught about the operation of natural laws in relationship to the life that you live. As you fit yourself by progress so greater knowledge comes to you.

"I, whom you call Silver Birch, represent only a small portion of the knowledge that belongs to the infinity of the spheres. As you grow, other teachers greater than I can use me to impart higher knowledge and wisdom to you."

"To save the world, must we broadcast this teaching to everybody?" asked Vernon.

"To save the world?" questioned Silver Birch. "The world must learn to perform its own salvation. There is no ready-made plan. There is no prepared, cut-and-dried system.

"Your world has to learn that, behind what it regards as the manifestation of life, there is the eternal reality of the spirit, that the children of matter are not only worldly beings but spiritual beings expressing themselves through bodies of matter.

"The bodies of matter must be as perfect as they can be made through having all the necessities of life freely at their disposal, as the Great Spirit would have them.

"Then their spirits must be freed from all dogmatic and credal trammels, so that they do not give allegiance to things that have no real or spiritual value, so that they work only for that which is true, so that the warring and the quarrelling and the strife over creeds and dogmas, which have held your world in chains for thousands of years, can be abolished.

"We preach the gospel of the spiritual brotherhood of all peoples, with the Great White Spirit as the common Father.

"What stands in the way is the earthly conception, the churches built on error, the usurping of privilege, the pride and the power of tyrants, petty tyrants who hold the whip hand."

When someone said "Thank you," Silver Birch, as usual, reminded those gathered that he must not be thanked, but that it was the Great Spirit to Whom gratitude should be expressed.

"We use the earth phrase out of habit," someone explained.

"I know, my son," replied the guide. "But if I did not always correct you and always draw attention to the laws of the Great Spirit, some would begin to pay us praise and to worship us, and then the same troubles would start once more."

Silver Birch then spoke, when asked which spirit friends were present, of the enormous number who regularly attended the sittings of the circle.

"There are as many as 5,000 people here tonight," he said.

"There are not only those you knew on earth, and those who are interested in the circle. There are those we bring to hear you talk, because they do not think that it is possible.

"Others are brought here so that they can learn how we come through to your world of matter, so that they can use other mediums in other parts of the world. There is a great missionary work, not only for your world but for our world too, for we do not sacrifice any time or power.

"The great lesson that those in my world have to learn is how to use spirit power in order to impress your minds. The great value of an understanding of these laws is that your minds become accessible.

"You do not realise how unknown to yourselves you are all the recipients of inspiration from the world of spirit.

"There are many in your world who are counted as great scientists, great inventors and great teachers. They are only the vehicles of intelligences from my world. It does not matter so long as the truth or the discovery is made known. Who receives the credit is of no account . . .

"Every experience has its advantage and disadvantage. The higher your soul evolves the greater is the progress it has made—but the more it knows there is to be evolved. That is its disadvantage, it is more dissatisfied. The more sensitive you become to beauty, the more sensitive you are to ugliness. The higher you rise, the lower you can sink.

"Life is shadow and sunlight, calm and storm. An even monotone is not life; life is composed of happiness and joy with occasional sadness, for it is only by having these extreme divergences that character can grow and experience come to the soul.

"That is why there is a lesson to be learned from sorrow, from the storm, from the bitterness of life. Sometimes those who are in the shadows rail against the Great Spirit because they do not understand that that experience is necessary to their own unfoldment, but sunshine is only to be truly appreciated if you have been in the shadows.

"Through comparison, the soul begins truly to live. If your experiences were limited only to that which you thought was good, happy and beautiful, life would be very empty, for it would possess no depth.

"The wise individual is the one who faces each new day with eagerness and steady resolve, determined to learn from all the experiences that await him the lessons that they all can teach to help him on the infinite road that leads to the Great Spirit."

Silver Birch devoted this particular sitting to answering the problems of the sitters. One wondered whether there was unlimited power at the disposal of spirit guides.

"The power we have is dependent on our own evolution and on the ability to receive and transmit," said the guide. "Our state of evolution determines the amount of power at our disposal. The instruments at our disposal determine the amount that can be poured through to your world. These are the factors which govern the receiving and the distributing of the power from our realms."

"Then there is unlimited power, if it can be used," commented the questioner.

"Yes," answered Silver Birch, "because power comes from the Infinite Spirit."

The circle member remarked that it seemed at seances that guides were always careful not to waste power, which would appear unnecessary if the supply were unlimited.

"When you are accustomed to manifestations," said the guide, "you know that if you go beyond a certain limit then the sitters will have to pay the price in depletion and loss of nervous energy and force. We do not wish to be placed in a position where we are accused of undermining the health of those who come to us seeking manifestations of the power of the spirit.

"In fact, the reverse is true and your health should improve, for power that is normally repressed is brought into circulation—and remember, too, that the power we bring from our world is the power of life-giving essence which invigorates."

It seemed that the seance was hardly half over when Silver Birch announced that the time was almost exhausted. But the sitters were wrong and the guide was right, for when the medium came out of trance it was found that only five minutes were left.

Before he went, Silver Birch said: "I have tried to show myself as your friend, guardian and guide. I wanted you to feel that I was near you, that whatever qualities I might possess they did not prevent me from enjoying a close personal touch with you, that I was interested in your problems and your difficulties and ready to give you personal help and guidance if I could.

"Remember, I am not only a teacher, seeking to teach eternal truths and reveal the powers of the spirit; I am also the friend of each one of you, for I love you dearly and strive always to help you with all the strength and power that I possess.

"Come to me always with your difficulties, no matter what they be. If I can help you, I will do so. If I cannot, I will strive to give you strength to bear whatever cross you may be called upon to carry."

'Through all our hearts'

"I pray to the Great White Spirit of all life that His radiance shall fill our beings and His light illumine our pathway, His love shall flow through all our hearts and His will shall become ours.

"I pray that the mighty power of His spirit shall be poured out upon us as we strive to bring into closer union the world of matter and the world of spirit, as we strive to clear away all the obstacles and limitations so that those who dwell in the world of matter may have a fuller understanding of life in all its eternal realities.

"We strive to restore that power of Thy spirit which has been revealed throughout all ages to those who had the clear sight and the clear hearing, the inspired prophets and seers, the wise men and women. We seek to reveal it in all its fullness, that its mighty power may stir the hearts, the minds and the souls and bring liberty and freedom to those who are still in the darkness of ignorance and slavery.

"We strive to bring the light of spiritual truth, spiritual wisdom and spiritual knowledge to those who need it, so that, encouraged, inspired, enthused from on high, they can strive for greater reform, to do away with all the injustices, the inequalities, all the barriers that prevent Thy children from inheriting Thy plenteous bounty which Thou hast given them in all Thy lavish generosity.

"We strive to oppose all vested interests that stand in the way of truth, freedom and justice, so that for all time there may be abolished from earth those dark blots of chaos, disease, misery and starvation which are no part of Thy plan but which are caused by the misused free will of those who have power and do not use it in Thy service.

"We labour to unite all people of good will, all those whose desire is to uplift and serve. We bring our message to all who are ready to receive it, striving to make Thy kingdom a reality in all planes of life.

"To this end we pray and we labour, asking that the power of Thy spirit shall guide us always and inspire us even to greater service. This is the prayer of Thy Indian servant, who seeks to serve."

Chapter Ten

'CREATION IS INFINITE'

A PRAISEWORTHY characteristic of Silver Birch was that no matter how difficult or obscure a subject put to him he always had at his command a superb and instant answer. Indeed, the beloved guide welcomed the points which some lesser beings might have dodged.

Journalist A. W. Austen, a circle member for some years, told of a remarkable question-and-answer session between this world and the next.

"What do you consider to be the most urgent reform that is necessary in the world?" Austen asked.

"That is a very hard question," Silver Birch admitted, "for all over your world there are injustices that cry out to be remedied. There are wrongs that shriek to be righted; there are so many pestilential blots on your civilisation that it is hard to know where to make a start. But the most urgent reform, as I see it, is to get rid of the needless poverty, desolation and misery which is the fate of countless thousands. When there is so much, that any should be denied the very fundamentals of a material existence is very wrong.

"The greatest reform that cries out for accomplishment is to redress the disparity between those who have too much and those who have not enough. How can you teach souls to find themselves when their poor, pitiable, emaciated physical bodies are not a fitting temple for the spirit of God to dwell therein? We are not blind to the prime necessities of your physical selves and our mission is to bring to your world those conditions of living which enable body, soul and mind to find the realities necessary for their existence in a state of happiness and well-being."

Next Austen asked the wise spirit teacher, "If you were a dictator what would be your first reform?" But Silver Birch would not even consider the possibility of his being a dictator.

"I cannot put myself in a position where I would have a world of puppets at my disposal," he said, "for that is contrary to the Law as I know it. It is not through dictatorships, through enforced commands which must be obeyed in fear and trembling lest dire punishment awaits, that peace, harmony and happiness can come to your world. You cannot set the world right by a series of ordinances that must be immediately obeyed. The chaos caused by years and years of confusion can only gradually become clarified and even then only through goodwill, the desire to be of real helpfulness imbuing all those who are the leaders of mankind.

"Neither I, nor any other who claims to be a spiritual teacher, could ever act as a dictator, for our whole mission is to awaken the slumbering conscience, to teach the dormant spirit to arise and claim the inherent gift of the Great Spirit that is its own. Only thus will true happiness and peace and concord come to your world. No one person on earth can reach that stage of perfection where he is entitled to rule over others and his words to be obeyed as implicit commands decreed by infallible authority."

Here Austen asked Silver Birch what he considered to be the most necessary step in Britain's relations with other countries.

"This country of yours has a great mission to perform, for it is destined to give a lead in bringing peace and also in staving off many of the disasters that threaten so many countries," answered the guide. "But it will have to remember that before there can be peace in your world there will have to be a spirit of self-sacrifice and service. Unless those who see with the eyes of discernment are prepared to make concessions, are prepared to give that which is not necessary for their own happiness and well-being but would enable other countries to find solutions to their problems—unless a lead is given in that direction, your country will fail in its mission.

"Some countries have too much; some have too little. You are rich in many things and where other countries are poor in those same things you could arrange a means of exchange that would enable problems to be solved without the shedding of blood. But there must be no arrogance, no dogged determination based upon obstinacy to say, 'What we have we hold.' Unless you are prepared to give, you cannot receive."

"Are you thinking of colonies?" Austen interposed.

"Yes, everything," he said. "The land, the sea, the air—those do not belong to countries; they belong to the Great Spirit of all life. His spirit is expressed in His children, and they should receive, as part of their natural heritage, all that is necessary for their well-being, their development, their unfoldment and their experience on earth, so that when they lay down their burdens when death comes they are ready to die, equipped, prepared for the greater life in the world of spirit."

Often Silver Birch spoke of a New World, one without war where a spirit of brotherhood would be expressed.

To Austen, this seemed "an optimistic view." His point was that the world would always contain those at varying stages of evolution. With the hope of clarifying the position, he asked Silver Birch if he agreed that "creation is continuous and that 'new' souls—as opposed to reincarnated souls—are constantly being born."

"The Great Spirit is infinite, and so the process of creation is infinite," he replied, "progressing always in its multitudinous expressions from imperfection to perfection, from immaturity to maturity, through all the countless grades of evolution. That process is timeless. It had no beginning, it has no end, for it belongs to infinity. It is part of the infinite

Great Spirit, and that self-same spirit finds its expression in human life at varying stages of unfoldment. But when you speak of 'new' souls, do you mean that something begins which had no existence before?"

"Yes," Austen confirmed.

"That is impossible," said Silver Birch, "for all life is based on preceding life. Life gives birth to life, constantly expressing itself in many forms. Spirit, unevolved because it has no earthly contact, finds expression in your world through suitable instruments fashioned by you, as you provide physical bodies commensurate with the spirit which has to use it so that it can possess that earthly education necessary for its evolution. It is new insofar as its earthly experience is concerned, but it is not new in the sense that it had no existence as spirit before it expressed itself on earth. Spirit is the stuff out of which all life is made; spirit is the primary substance of creation; spirit, as spirit, has always existed and will always exist.

"That excludes, of course, those who return to earth for further experience. But, omitting those who reincarnate and dealing only with those who incarnate for the first time, they had no individuality, no human consciousness before their physical expression. Human consciousness only begins with earthly expression. It is the body of matter that supplies the vital link which enables the spirit to become aware of itself as individual consciousness."

Austen asked the guide whether he would hazard an opinion on the proportion of "new" to "old" souls among those who are being born.

"It is impossible to give any answer to your question that would be even approximately correct," he replied. "But I would say the proportion is fairly equal."

"In that case," said Austen, "there will always be on earth those who are more evolved and those who are less evolved."

"Yes," agreed the guide, "otherwise evolution would not be taking place. Try to understand that life, because it is life, cannot ever be static, for that way lies stagnation. Life is rhythm, motion, progress, unfoldment, development, the reaching out towards perfection all the time. Unless there were constant gradations of life, unless there was a constant pilgrimage on the rungs of the ladder of progress, life would not be life. It is in the variety of evolution, with its multitudinous stages of development, that life becomes life.

"If all were at the same stage, if perfection were attained, if there were no necessity for further striving, no need for new attainments, no need for still greater expression, then the incentive to live, to achieve, would gradually become extinct. The motivation of life is always onward, striving to reach out to clasp that which is at present beyond its grasp. And it is always in the striving, in the attempt to conquer, seeking to triumph over difficulty, that the spirit finds itself and God is at work amongst you."

Arising from the spirit answers, Austen wanted to know whether less evolved souls would always cause trouble in the world and retard progress.

"Yes, but always remember this, that what you call unevolved souls are really unevolved by comparison with those who are more evolved," said the guide. "As your standard becomes higher, so you recognise that those you considered were evolved are not so evolved as you thought they were. All the difficulties of your world, and indeed those belonging to the lower strata of my life, are caused wholly and solely by selfishness, greed, avarice, self-interest in all its expressions.

"There will be always some less evolved than others. How else would you have it? Would you have all humanity reaching the same stage of evolution at the same time? Would you have every human being moulded to the same pattern at the same point of progress at the same time? Would you reduce all life to a state of monotonous equality in regard to its development? Would you have only light and no shade? Would you have only sunshine and no storm? Would you have only virtue and no wickedness? Would you have laughter and no tears? How would you regulate your world unless it be through an infinite variety of expression?"

Austen suggested to Silver Birch that, in view of the many differences in evolution that must always be present, his description of the New World seemed to be too optimistic.

"No, the New World is born," the guide declared, "born in agony of birth, with a baptism of tears and misery and sadness. But the New World is here. Its rays are beginning to pierce the fog of your world. But even in this New World all will not have been achieved. There will be plenty to remedy, to improve, to strengthen. There will still be weakness to be overcome, there will still be troubles to be eradicated. But there will be a new basis for life. Much of the needless misery, much of the needless deprivation, much of the needless starvation and sadness will have gone. The basis of life will be changed, for gradually selfishness will be overthrown and service will reign in its place."

"But is it not true that we shall only get what we deserve?" Austen queried.

"Yes, the New World will come more quickly or more slowly, as more of you help us or hinder us in our efforts to co-operate with you," said Silver Birch. "You will not get more than you deserve or less than you deserve, for so perfect is natural law in its expression that its scales are always evenly balanced. They are weighted down neither on one side nor the other. I tell you of conditions that are operating and, as they continue to operate, what will be changed. Do not forget that you will reap in your world the harvest of countless generations of labour wrought by many pioneers, idealists and reformers, who made sacrifices to advance the lot of mankind."

To Austen it seemed unfair that some "new" souls should be born into conditions that were far better than those into which other "new" souls had similarly been born. Could Silver Birch explain the apparent injustice?

"They will be born into a better world, but more will be expected of them in consequence," he said, "for they will not have to fight the fights that others have had to win in days gone by. It is purely a matter of comparison. Remember this always, no man cheats the laws of the Great Spirit. At no time can you alter in any way by one hair's breadth what you deserve. Reward and punishment are fixed and immutable, determined only by your conduct in your life. There is no favouritism, there is no evasion. Divine justice is perfect in its expression. You will find that you will receive just what you have earned—not one whit more, not one whit less."

"That is how we ought to want it," Austen commented.

"That is how men and women of courage should desire it," said Silver Birch, "not to have rewards they have not earned or punishments they have not deserved. You should be prepared to endure the punishments that you deserve and carry upon your shoulders the responsibilities that you have created. It was all said in the Bible—'Be not deceived, God is not mocked, for what a man sows that he will reap.' And I cannot say it any better than that.

"The laws that are made in your world may favour some unduly and punish others needlessly. There may be privileges that come because of rank or title or high position. But these will not obtain in the world of spirit. Every allowance will be made. The soul will register just that stage of attainment that it has reached by its life in your world—no higher, no lower. Just what you have made yourself to be, that you will be when death calls you to another life."

Next Austen asked Silver Birch what should be the attitude

to spiritual or divine guidance received by individuals who sit alone in the silence.

"There is no spirit, however exalted, in my world who would desire you to accept his teachings without consideration, without pondering and without reflection," he replied. "We do not desire automatons who will mechanically perform all that is said. Our mission is to increase your own sense of responsibility, to stimulate the divine that is within you, to enable you to have even greater command over your reasoning faculties. God speaks to you through your soul, but He also speaks to you through your mind. Whilst it is true that the kingdom of heaven is within, the mind is also God's kingdom—or should be.

"Never do anything which your reason rejects. Enthrone reason as your guide. We would never suggest to you that you perform tasks that are foreign to your common sense. Ours is a mission of co-operation. We strive to make you aware of the infinite qualities that you possess, many of them so dormant that they never find expression. We want you to find yourselves, your real selves, so that you may order your lives in such a fashion that the Great Spirit is expressed through you. If you receive promptings, if you receive what seem to be messages in the silence that urge tasks upon you, do not perform them if your common sense objects. Only those who have reached a certain standard of spiritual attainment can be sure of the prompting that comes to them in the silence.

"It is better that you work with us, once you have learned to trust us and are convinced that our mission is to serve you and through you to serve humanity. We have striven to demonstrate that we are experienced in the knowledge of spiritual laws, that ours is a divine mission that seeks always to bring the richness of spiritual truth within your grasp. Is it not better that you should co-operate with known intelligences of proved worth rather than that alone, unguided, you should seek to penetrate what is the unknown? What would your answer be?"

Austen told the guide he considered it always to be better to know with whom one is speaking.

"That is so," said Silver Birch. "When the teacher has proved his ability to teach, why not utilise his services that are freely offered you? When a soul has reached the stage of development when he is aware of all who seek to inspire him and to commune with him from the world of spirit, then there are no difficulties to be overcome. But all humanity is at different stages of evolution."

Still the two-world debate continued. Austen admitted that to him it seemed there was a limit to the sacredness of life. Taking it to an extreme, it seemed to him "foolish to suggest that the life of a germ is sacred if by sparing it we endanger the life of a human being." Would the spirit mentor enlighten him on this point?

"Where does consciousness begin?" asked Silver Birch. "Has the germ consciousness? Has a snake consciousness? Has a flea consciousness? Has a microbe consciousness? They have not in the sense that you understand consciousness, the awareness of oneself. Consciousness is the knowledge of what you are, who you are, what you could be. That consciousness is not resident in germs. Where there is conscious life you have creation at work, and it is wrong for you to interfere with that consciousness and to prevent it from having the fullness of expression in your world to which it is entitled."

This answer did not satisfy Austen who reminded the guide that animals did not possess consciousness as defined, but we were taught it was wrong to kill them.

"Below individual consciousness, in the animal life there is a group consciousness," he said. "Below animals, the group consciousness ceases to function. There is no consciousness in a germ."

"Is the germ capable of feeling pain?" asked Austen.

"No," said Silver Birch.

"Then are we to be guided by whether pain is involved in killing?" was the next question.

"The guide is consciousness," said Silver Birch. "Where there is consciousness, it is wrong to kill. You should allow the fullest freedom to all human beings to enjoy life in all its expressions, so that its richness may reach them and equip them for death, the liberator into the world of spirit. But because your world is a changing world, you are often compelled to interfere with the rights of others because you desire to help them. Your motive, sincerely, honestly and truthfully, is to serve.

"I say that because of vivisection. To me, that is wrong. It is often cruel and it is needless and it fails also to achieve its object. But I know that there are many who perform vivisection, not because they wish to inflict cruelty on animals, but only because their desire is to help humanity. They think that they can gain knowledge which will help them in their conquering of disease. Their motive is sincere.

"But where there is needless killing, where there is slaughter of animals solely to satisfy human appetites, where beautiful birds are shot in the name of sport—then there can be no justification. Life is sacred, life is of the Great Spirit. When life becomes conscious and takes human—and even, in its lower stage, animal form—it should be entitled to be treated with sacredness. Life should not be held cheaply, for life is the Great Spirit in expression. You have no power to create life, therefore you should not seek to destroy its means of expression.

"Realise this, that when we are asked questions to which there can be no answer of 'Yes' or 'No,' we do try honestly to give you a point of view that will help. I have no desire to be arbitrary, I only want to be of service. It may be that you could find apparent contradictions in answers given at different times, but then we are dealing with different phases of the subject.

"And remember also I make no claim to infallibility. I do not say that I have reached the limit of all knowledge and wisdom. I, like you, am human still. I, too, strive after perfection. I, too, have weaknessess to conquer. I, too, have progress to achieve. I do not say that what I tell you represents final truth. I only tell you what I know and, if I do not know, what I believe. If the views that I express cause disagreement, that is all to the good, for then we can reason with one another. You can add your stock of wisdom to mine and in considering these problems we can learn from one another and help one another to a greater understanding.

"Co-operation does not only mean that we should try to help you, but that you should also try to help us. I do not want it to be assumed that at any stage, when a problem arises, you say, 'Consult Silver Birch, consult Red Cloud, consult White Hawk, and what they say is final.' That is not so. We will give you the knowledge at our disposal, but remember we make no claim to infallibility. If we fail to stimulate you into thinking for yourselves, then we have failed in our mission."

At this juncture, Austen suggested to Silver Birch that to some the knowledge of life after death might tend to cheapen life on earth: they might consider that if life could not be destroyed there was less harm than they previously thought in killing.

"Have we not always taught that increasing knowledge brings increasing responsibilities?" asked the guide. "Because you have this knowledge, you have a greater responsibility in the way you use it. Your standard of life must be higher because of knowledge and, if it is not, then you yourself will pay the price. You cannot cheat. You cannot pretend once knowledge is vouchsafed to you. Once you understand the

Plan, and the pattern of life has been made clear to you, it should give you an increasing responsibility of your duty to your neighbour, to your world and to yourself. Life should be richer, more sacred, and the desire to serve should burn brightly within you.

"If knowledge does not do that for you, then you do not possess it. It has passed you by, for if you fail to apply truth when you know truth, your spirit is impoverished and you are the sufferer. The laws of the Great Spirit cannot be cheated, not even by philosophical quibbles. What you call Spiritualism should make you aware of your place in the scheme of life. If it does not, you have not learned its lessons and must pay the price. Do not blame truth if you do not understand it. Blame yourself, for truth is still true even though it has not penetrated through to you. Truth is not altered by argument. Because it is truth, it is true."

When Austen similarly interviewed White Eagle, the guide of Bertha Hirst, he could not explain to Austen the tie between people and their guardian angels, as he confessed he had never considered the question. So Austen asked Silver Birch whether he could answer it.

"It is a tie of spiritual affinity," he said. "Sometimes that happens when there is a blood relationship, oft-times it happens when there is no blood relationship at all. Wherever there is a mutual interest, based upon the tie of affinity between kindred spirits, then the guardian or guide—call it what name you like—is able to render service because the attraction is there. The greater the bond of spiritual affinity, the closer is the proximity between the guardian and its charge."

Remembering that Silver Birch had said earlier in the interview that individual consciousness does not exist before the soul is incarnated into matter, Austen wondered how it could have developed characteristics sufficient to create a spiritual affinity.

"That is something that is so hard to express in your earthly language," said the guide. "There is a bond that can be determined from the moment of conception. The tiny germ cells that, when they coalesce, provide the physical vehicle of life, possess within themselves all the qualities that later find expression in the mature earthly body. So, too, does the spirit possess in miniature the spiritual qualities that will also find expression."

"Did that mean that our evolution was determined insofar as we had to evolve along certain individual lines but could choose our own rate of evolution?" Austen asked.

"Certain things are fixed, by virtue of the body at your command and by the spirit that incarnates into that body," said Silver Birch. "Irrespective of rebirth, the law that determines the invasion of that body by spirit also to a large extent determines the expression. I do not want that to be construed into saying that everything is predestined, but in a world of law human life conforms to law. There are variations, but in the main much has to be fixed.

"The rate of evolution depends essentially on the free will of the individual, but obviously there are limits within that earthly incarnation. That depends upon the use he makes of opportunity, but he is limited, for example, to the extent that he could not achieve perfection. There is a quality in the spirit that is known to advanced souls in our world, and the appointment of a guardian is dependent upon the affinity of spiritual interest between them."

"Do you mean that guardians are appointed by somebody else, and it is not a choice of a charge by the guardian?" Austen queried, probing further.

"Yes, they are appointed always," said Silver Birch. "There is law in my world, much more rigidly than in yours. The harmony between them is determined because the qualities are known at the beginning. The headmaster of a school, if he knew the latent qualities of all the children entrusted to his charge, and knew the capabilities of the teachers he had, would know which children should be under the tutorship of each teacher. Unfortunately, the factors are not always known in your world—but they are in ours."

'Thy wisdom guides all'

"Let us seek the blessing of the Great Spirit of all. Oh, Great White Spirit, the whole of creation pays homage to Thee, because Thy laws sustain every manifestation of life and all rhythm is but an expression of Thee. Oh, Great Spirit, Thou art the centre of all life, whether it be the life that is expressed in the highest heights of spirit or in the lowest depths of matter. Thou dost embrace all, for Thy wisdom guides all.

"Thou hast sent into the world of matter at all times instruments who can radiate Thy love, Thy wisdom and Thy knowledge, that they might become living demonstrations of Thy spirit, to bring the light of Thy truth into the darkness of men's minds, to illumine all mankind with the rays of Thy infinite wisdom and love.

"Oh, Great Spirit, Thou hast sent us as Thy messengers, once again to bring to the children of earth the knowledge of Thee and of Thy laws, that they may understand their relationship with Thee, and so begin to understand themselves and the purpose for which Thou hast placed them in the world of matter.

"We thank Thee because we are able to hold communion with those susceptible to the things of Thy spirit and whose ears, eyes, minds, hearts and souls are attuned to our larger life and who can listen to the message that Thou wouldst have us proclaim."

Chapter Eleven

'AS YOUR SOULS UNFOLD'

SADLY, Silver Birch never revealed his true identity. What we do know is that he was certainly an exalted spirit being who merely used the astral body of a North American Indian in order to communicate. Once, however, he explained that when on earth "I venerated many gods."

At the sitting in question the guide began by saying that some said a little knowledge "is a dangerous thing. Sometimes a lot of knowledge can be very dangerous, especially if people learn the wrong things.

"When their learning fills their brains, it does not give their minds a chance to operate through the grey matter. I feel sorry for those 'men of God' who have so much to unlearn. They have built a structure based on shifting sands and they try to defend their sandy castles against the onslaught of spirit truths.

"They have built falsely. They have surrounded the Nazarene with fable. They have magnified him into the Great Spirit of Life and, because the foundation is a faulty one, they have gradually to destroy it. As they destroy, fear strikes their hearts.

"They think there can be nothing left at all, whereas the truth is that, if they had built on the foundation of fact, of natural law, there would be nothing to destroy.

"That is why we have come back to your world—to ask you to give no obedience to any one man, to any one book, to any one church, to any leader, to any being whether in the world of matter or in the world of spirit, but only to learn obedience to the laws of the Great Spirit, for they alone are infallible and unerringly right.

"That is why we preach the natural laws, and the natural laws only. If you call that Spiritualism it does not matter, as long as what you understand embraces the natural laws of the Great Spirit and their operation throughout all the spheres of life, whether life that is visible to you or life as it is known in the planes of spirit.

"Your world has set its store by leaders, and has magnified them out of their true importance, and so it has created difficulties of theology—difficulties with scientists, with philosophers and with all those honest people who want their minds to be free and who cannot accept anything which makes their reason revolt.

"That is why we emphasise the laws of the Great Spirit, for the true understanding of these laws harmonises all knowledge. They cannot in any way cause the minds of scientists, philosophers, free-thinkers or anybody to revolt, for they are founded upon eternal, unalterable, immutable operations of the Great Spirit.

"You see the wisdom of the counsel that is given to us to express. As your world grows in wisdom and understanding, its people will learn to regulate their lives according to the laws of the Great Spirit. They will learn to have obedience to the Law.

"They will learn that all the misery and the starvation, the suffering and the heartbreaks that come through your worldly conditions are all caused because the law is not obeyed.

"When the fuller understanding comes, there will be swept away all the hideous growths in the garden of the Great Spirit that prevent its beauty being shown to every one of His children.

"With that aim we strive, not only to make the souls of mankind free, not only to liberate their minds, but to give their bodies of matter a chance to live in harmony with the laws of the Great Spirit."

Then Silver Birch gave an indication of the progress that he has had to make since leaving the earth . . . nearly 3,000 years ago.

"It took me many years to learn to think like that," he said, "for in my days on earth I venerated many gods. I had to learn that there is only one Great Spirit, Who has provided eternal laws for the control of every phase of life throughout the boundless universe.

"As our teaching grows in your world, it will mean the end of all separateness between people. It will mean the end of national barriers. It will mean the end of race distinctions, class distinctions, colour distinctions and all the distinctions between churches and chapels, temples, mosques and synagogues, for gradually all will learn that they have a part of the Great Spirit's truth and that the part enshrined in the heart of every other religion in no way contradicts that portion which is precious to them.

"So, out of the apparent confusion, the divine pattern will take its shape and harmony and peace will come. I tell you these things, so that you can understand part of the great Plan, the part that we who return from the world of spirit play in it, and the part that each one of you must play in it before your earthly course is run."

Around the same time, Silver Birch rejected the Orthodox idea that the resurrection of Jesus was a miracle. Fittingly, his words came at an Easter sitting.

"Your Christian world pays its tribute to one who rose from the 'dead,' who was seen after his 'death,' who demonstrated that life continues beyond 'death,'" said the spirit sage.

"The Nazarene demonstrated that he was the same individual and he gave as proofs, in the materialised body, the

earthly marks of the crucifixion. After that, he revealed
himself again.

"Your Christian world believes all that, though it cannot
prove it. But it says it was a miracle!

"We have returned through the same laws to demonstrate
the life beyond 'death,' to show that the Great Spirit is eternal
and the operation of His laws immutable, that even as one was
resurrected so are all resurrected, because resurrection is a law
of the Great Spirit of life."

One sitter asked if the resurrection occurred "as recorded in
the Gospels?"

"Almost," replied Silver Birch.

"Was the stone actually moved?"

"Yes."

"Why was that necessary?"

"That was only a symbol."

"What happened to the physical body of Jesus?" asked the
sitter.

"It was dematerialised," was the reply . . .

"Whether the manifestation of the Spirit is seen or heard
does not matter very much.

"What is more important is the unfolding of your own
souls' power, for, as you sit here week after week, so you are
attuning yourselves to higher vibrations and becoming more
accessible to the wisdom of the ages, which, although it has
evolved and is evolving, is always waiting to pour itself down
into your world of matter, to obey the law of service. But it
must find instruments attuned to its vibrations.

"And, as your souls unfold and you rise higher and higher
in the scale of vibrations, so you come into closer touch with
higher and greater spiritual forces, that are not seen or heard
but which belong to the eternal realities of the Spirit.

"That is the reality of your lives. So much of your time is
spent in chasing the shadows, in trying to capture the illusion,

in trying to secure the ephemeral. In silence, in harmony and in love, your souls unfold all the time. Though it may be slow, it is sure and certain.

"The Great Spirit that is within each one of you unfolds and evolves, and you are able to express more and more of its divinity, because you have all met together in one place and with one accord.

"The Nazarene told you, many years ago, that, where two or three are gathered together, there is the Great Spirit to pour down His blessing. We teach the same truths, but they reject us.

"Truths do not change. Men's minds change, but truth is constant because it is based upon knowledge, and knowledge comes from the Great Spirit. He is the centre and the source of all inspiration. It is all so simple and so easy to understand, but your world has made it so very difficult."

Silver Birch referred to the Nazarene again before attending another spirit-world conference. He spoke "of the joys that belong to greater spheres and the radiant beings who are behind this great work of ours, the teachers and the leaders of many nations who, through centuries of progress and unfoldment, have now earned the right to direct us all.

"More than all these things," he added, "I wish that you could see and hear the Nazarene and feel that great love as he encourages us in our missions, as he expresses his knowledge of all that has been done and urges us to go forward with new strength, with new hope, with new vision and with new purpose. He is not the Nazarene of the Churches—exalted into a deified place—but a great spirit who strives still to serve through many instruments.

"For a short time I shall be in the spheres where I lived for many years, to feel once again that vitalising power of the spirit, so invigorating in its strength, so beautiful in all its fullness, making you realise what life is when you are able to experience it in the higher realms of spirit. We speak with all humility and with no pride at all . . .

"If all the beautiful paintings of the world, all the inspired visions and all the great artistry that you have ever heard of in your world of matter and all the deepest and greatest beauties of nature were all combined into one whole object it would be but a very pale reflection of life in the higher regions."

Silver Birch mentioned the recompense for his work, how he saw "the increasing spread of our knowledge" and realised that the mission of the guides was succeeding in many places and how "we are able to transmit the truths which have been so long forgotten and are now being restored in your midst.

"I am proud that because of our efforts we have accomplished so much throughout the world of matter . . . Hearts that were once sad are now a little more joyful. Light has pierced the gloom of darkness. Now, there is a little more knowledge where before there was ignorance. We have aided those who have become faint-hearted, given strength to those who were weary, guided those who had lost their way and acted as an incentive to those who strive to work for their fellows, giving them the realisation that behind them there is a mighty host of spirit spurring them on in all their endeavours for the Great Spirit and His children.

"And I am also happy that I have been able to bring to you some of those you love and who love you, so that you may realise more than you ever did before that you have never lost them, that 'death' does not divide but brings together those whom love and affection and friendship have made one in heart and soul.

"I wish you could see the extent of our influence. We have helped to break barriers, to remove obstacles and to bring knowledge. These are the things your world needs, the simple truths that will enable spiritual, mental, and material freedom to come to your world.

"As you know, we live only to serve, for through service and service alone can your world be saved from itself . . .

"Do not think only in terms of the power of the Spirit in the past. Remember that the power which operated through the Nazarene is operating once again.

"Just as those who were the leaders of the churches in that time rejected that power of the Spirit, and said it was of the Devil, so once again they reject the same power of the Spirit as it operates today. But your world has evolved, for they do not crucify any longer.

"The splendour of the Nazarene does not belong only to the past, but to the present. Where do you think he is today? Do you think the story of his life ended in Jerusalem? Where do you think his great spirit would be today, with your world of matter full of distress, trouble and bitterness?

"Those who deny us and say we preach the gospel of darkness are in line with the same people who, in the days gone by, made the same accusation against the Nazarene. We come with the same power of the Great Spirit, bringing the same manifestations of the Spirit, the same message, 'Comfort the mourner, heal the sick, bring light to those who are in darkness, health to the afflicted, strength to the weary, knowledge to the ignorant.'

"We are all the servants of the Great Spirit. Some of us have evolved a little higher. Because of that, we return to give service, for service is the law of life. Where there is no service, there is desolation. Where there is service, there is peace and happiness. Your world must build a new system of life with service to one another.

"It is all very simple, but they make it so hard."

Answering another point raised at a different home circle meeting, the guide stated:

"Yours is a strange world, and when you view it with eyes that do not belong to matter you marvel at the folly of the people who live in it. They set such store over their puny possessions, which crumble into the dust, and they neglect the priceless treasures of the Spirit which are eternal.

"They have no understanding of spiritual values. They live for the moment, for the fleeting pleasures and the joys, and their souls, so covered over with material desires, seldom are able to express the divinity that is within.

"And yet, in your world, they are counted as intelligent because they have accumulated temporary possessions. Who is the intelligent one—the man who strives to build that which must perish, or the one who strives to build that which will endure?"

"Jesus said that," commented one of the sitters, recalling the parable of the houses built on sand and on rock.

"Yes," was the reply, "he also said something about treasures in heaven, where the moth and the rust cannot corrupt. But your world has forgotten the Nazarene, and those who profess to serve him have themselves built material possessions and set store by the things of matter.

"Not all of them, for here and there a mighty urge to serve fires with burning zeal the soul that is ready to uplift others, not for self but only for another."

"How do the people on your side pour the healing spirit through a healer?" was the next question. "Is it because he has a different kind of organism from other people?"

Silver Birch, in replying, pointed out that he was only referring to spiritual healers as apart from those who practise magnetic and other forms.

"You all have qualities of soul," he said, "and these qualities are nearer expression in some people than they are in others. As you strive for unfoldment, that quality, the psyche, the spiritual, call it what you will, unfolds and there is a closer co-operation between the instrument and the guides who work with him.

"The attunement is higher, finer and closer. The rays blend into one state of beauteous harmony and, when that stage reaches its zenith, the whole band of my world and the instrument of yours become as one in unity.

"The nearer you are to that state of achievement, the higher and the greater and more powerful rays that belong to our spheres can be used through the band of guides and the instrument."

'The joys which are mine'

"With tears of sadness at leaving you, yet with joy in my heart at what awaits me, I leave you all," declared Silver Birch at the conclusion of one seance.

The "tears of sadness" were real, not merely a polite phrase, for when his medium came out of trance the tears were streaming down his face.

"Tonight is very solemn for us all," said the guide. "I do not like to come to say farewell, and yet I have to. I do not like to leave you and yet I know that, when I have gone, I return to where there is much rejoicing.

"How I wish I could take you all with me, so that your eyes may behold some of the beauties which are hidden from you, that you may see some of the realities of the world of spirit, so that you might meet some of the wise ones who strive to co-operate with you.

"But, alas, I cannot. I take you part of the way, but unfortunately you cannot retain in that consciousness which you express in the world of matter the memory of what you behold.

"You who dwell in bodies of flesh, and who are limited in your expression by five poor senses, do not know what it is to be free in spirit.

"You do not realise what it is to enjoy the precious liberty of the spirit, to see the beauty of the greater world, to enjoy its life, its dazzling sights and sounds, its poetry, its music, its love.

"I am sad to go, but that is where I belong. I shall taste for a few days the joys which are mine. I have your love which is very precious to me, which flows from your hearts and binds us all together and makes us one in unity.

"I feel that love flowing towards me and I strive to give you all the love that I possess.

"Now, for a little while, farewell to you," he concluded. "Raise your hearts in thanksgiving to the Great Spirit for the knowledge which has been vouchsafed to you.

"Be thankful for the privilege you enjoy. Try to make yourselves accessible to higher spheres of inspiration. Fill yourselves with the mighty power of the Spirit.

"Reach out to the Great Spirit of all. Fill your hearts with His love and your minds with His knowledge and wisdom.

"Attune yourselves to His will. Become at one with the Great Spirit and His laws. Live in rhythm and harmony with their operation in the world of matter."

The Silver Birch Books

Teachings of Silver Birch	first published in 1938
Guidance from Silver Birch	first published in 1966
Philosophy of Silver Birch	first published in 1969
More Philosophy of Siver Birch	first published in 1979
Light from Silver Birch	first published in 1983
Silver Birch Companion	first published in 1986
A Voice in the Wilderness	first published in 1986
The Seed of Truth	first published in 1987
The Spirit Speaks	first published in 1988
Lift Up Your Hearts	first published in 1990
The Universe of Silver Birch	first published in 1994
The Silver Birch Book of Questions and Answers	first published in 1998

The Spiritual Truth Press is the publishing arm of
The Spiritual Truth Foundation which is a charity
established to assist needy Spiritualists and Medium
as well as to help to spread spiritual truths by financing
the publication of new and classic books on subjects relevant
to our understanding of man's nature and destiny.

All proceeds from the sale of this book will go to the
Foundation to further its work. To that end it welcomes
donations and bequests.

For further information about The Spiritual Truth
Foundation contact the Secretary at 15 Broom Hall,
Oxshott, Surrey KT22 0JZ